MEGA
Success
Secrets

by Paul Skulitz

Paul Skulitz
paul@mega10success.com
877.767.3551

Prepared and Published by:

Faithful Life Publishers • North Fort Myers, FL 33903
www.FaithfulLifePublishers.com
info@FLPublishers.com

17 16 15 14 13 12 11   1 2 3 4 5 6

TABLE OF CONTENTS

PREFACE

I am truly glad you decided to read Mega Success Secrets and would like to begin by telling you why I decided to write this book.

One of the biggest problems entrepreneurs run into is marketing and finding the right people to join them in their opportunity. Like many of you, I have spent years in network marketing looking for a solution to my problems.

Mega Success Secrets offers solutions I found and will teach you network marketing skills where the more valuable you become to others, the more they will seek you out. I want to share a few of my past experiences, setbacks, and successes of my personal and network marketing experiences.

I am a caring individual and do not like to see my story of struggles and failure repeated on and on by others. Looking back, I wish my up-line would have shared their secrets with me because my journey would have been less frustrating knowing what struggles and failures were part of the process.

I always wanted to offer a solution as well as expertise but I didn't have the right tools, support, or knowledge to consider myself the "go to" person with answers pertaining to their particular question.

I knew other people shared the same state of mind as I did. Through network marketing I came across a group of people who had the same mindset of offering a solution to their marketing problems and forming a partnership to impact and inspire others to reach their goals.

The good thing about our group is that we all have a different expertise. We share our knowledge and information, teach each other, and work as a team to help develop other people to become the very best leaders where people will be knocking on their doors.

Now that leads me to my two-year study of why people spend money to get started in a business and then quit after a few months.

For two years I went back to people that joined my business or one of my associates businesses. I asked them why they joined only to quit that business in a few months. I found a lot of people joined out of excitement and hope that they would be a business owner but that dream never became a reality. Unfortunately, people in this industry have never been business owners. The discipline and skills necessary for success in network marketing is a whole new skill.

When people come into this industry they have the "sell" mentality not realizing people do not buy products, they buy people.

I had a mission….

I had to change people's mindset, I had to take ACTION!!!

Building a successful network marketing business is plain and simple — it is all about networking, building relationships, and creating value to others in the world.

When I confronted distributors with how they approach a potential customer/business builder, they always lead with the product and not with themselves.

When I have a new prospect, my conversation is about them never about me, my product or service. Eventually, as we are all human, they will ask you about yourself. That is your time to give a little bit of information but direct the conversation back to your potential customer.

Most people do not know how to market. They assume marketing is about "my product is better than yours," "we have the best compensation plan," "my product is cheaper," or "my product has a patent." None of these matters!!! No matter what the product or service, unless you knew how to market it to the right people, you will not make a dime. The money is not in the product — it is in knowing how to market. If people do not have the skill set to know how to market correctly, they give up quickly.

I was very fortunate to have a father who taught me to not ever give up. That lesson has gone with me through my whole life; I have had ups and downs, but I never gave up. My father was right — things will always work out if you never give up.

Here's an example. At the age of 22, I owned my own security alarm company. I was installing an alarm bell outside, and I was too lazy to get the ladder off the truck. I was almost done for the day and wanted to go home, so I hung out an upstairs window to install the alarm. As I was screwing in the alarm, the screwdriver slipped out of my hand. When I reached to catch it, I fell from the third story window and broke my back. The doctor told my wife and me that I was paralyzed from the waist down and I would not be able to walk again. That was a shock to us, but I said I will walk and I will live a normal life. After 18 months of saying to myself I would walk, I started to move my feet, and slowly I started to move my legs. Within six months from that point, I was walking. The doctor was shocked but did say that I would have back problems and I would still not be able to do what I did before. Within one year I was doing everything I ever did and better. Now at 61, I know that I broke my back but I still do everything I want to do and as good as anyone else. Now that is not giving up. So hearing someone say to me they are not interested in my business is nothing, I just move on to the next person.

In this book you will learn the secrets about how to be a successful networker. You will get valuable knowledge that can help you get what you want.

Set yourself apart from the masses and don't pitch your product or service, offer high quality information, build relationships, gain trust, and you will be surprised how fast your following will grow.

Everything lies within you; never give up.

Look adversity in the eye and go for it!!

You can change your life if you take all of the information and put it to good use.

After you are a successful network marketer and proud of it, do me one favor — contact me. I would love to hear from you. Your success is my success!!

Do you feel empowered? If so, let's get started!!

God Bless.

Chapter One

WHAT IS NETWORK MARKETING?

Definition – Multi-level marketing (MLM) is a form of network marketing (however, the terms are often used interchangeably). It is a marketing strategy that compensates promoters of direct selling companies not only for product sales they personally generate, but also for the sales of others they introduced to the company. The products and company are usually marketed directly to consumers and potential business partners by means of relationship referrals and word-of-mouth marketing.

Independent, unsalaried salespeople of multi-level marketing, referred to as distributors (or associates, independent business owners, dealers, franchise owners, sales consultants, consultants, independent agents, etc.), represent the parent company and are awarded a commission based upon the volume of product sold through each of their independent businesses (organizations).

Independent distributors develop their organizations by either building an active customer base, who buy direct from the parent company, or by recruiting a downline of independent distributors who also build a customer base, by expanding the overall organization.

Additionally, distributors can also earn a profit by retailing products they purchased from the parent company at wholesale price.

Distributors earn a commission based on the sales efforts of their organization, which includes their independent sales efforts as well as the leveraged sales efforts of their downline. This arrangement is similar to franchise arrangements where royalties are paid from the sales of individual franchise operations to the franchisor as well as to an area or region manager. Commissions are paid to multi-level marketing distributors according to the company's compensation plan. Multiple levels of people can receive royalties from one person's sales.

HISTORY OF NETWORK MARKETING

To know where we are going, it is beneficial to know where we came from. The most current history of network marketing began in the 1950s with Dr. Forrest Shacklee, who created Nutralite. Then the two biggest distributors, Jay Van Andel and Rich Devos, decided to venture out on their own. They started AMWAY. The corporation began by selling vitamins. They were so successful that they ended up buying the vitamin company. When multi-level marketing, usually referred to as MLM, first got started, there were very few players in the field. For this reason some of the first companies grew by leaps and bounds. These first companies had excellent products, but the compensation plans were not that great. They had tremendous volume requirements and staying qualified required one to jump through hoops. Most of these companies still exist and have not varied much from their original marketing methods.

Some of the first companies offered household products or cosmetics and personal care items. These products worked out fine because people were already spending money on these items anyway. The idea of purchasing these items through your own personal business appealed to people and the growth that followed was astounding.

Distinguishing legal and reputable MLMs from illegal pyramid or Ponzi schemes is sometimes difficult. MLM businesses operate in the United States in all 50 states and in more than 100 other countries, and new businesses may use terms like "affiliate marketing" or "home-based business franchising." However, many pyramid schemes try to present themselves as legitimate MLM businesses.

In most legitimate MLM companies, commissions are earned only on sales of the company's products or services. That is why here at Mega Success Secrets people make commissions on selling our product, and that product is eBook TRAINING. No money may be earned from recruiting alone ("sign-up fees"), though money earned from the sales of members recruited is one attraction of MLM arrangements. If participants are paid primarily from money received from new recruits, or if they are required to buy more product than they are likely to sell, then the company may be a pyramid or Ponzi scheme, which is illegal in most countries.

Just as one who plants a garden can expect weeds, scam artists did not take long to see the opportunity to get in on the band wagon. Pyramid schemes started to pop up everywhere, to the point that the government had to get involved. Things got so bad that the public started to refer to all multi-level marketing companies as pyramid schemes. The news was filled with lawsuits and companies being shut down. Some of these con artists made off with millions, and people who got involved with the companies lost a lot of money in many cases.

After having success in shutting down some companies that were clearly pyramid schemes, the government decided to go after some of the big well-established companies because, on the surface, the companies looked the same. The government attacked some billion dollar companies, who had the resources to hire the best attorneys and prove their legitimacy to operate just as any other business. The lawsuits went on for a few years, the government lost, and if you know anything about the industry, these companies are still major players.

Soon after the government backed off, other new multi-level marketing companies started to spring up. Most of these companies had excellent products, and the concept had already caught on. In the past an individual could sign up by filling out a form and mailing it to the company. With the Internet, one can pull up the website, sign up online, and be in business with their first order on the way in minutes instead of days.

Today, so many multi-level marketing companies exist that individuals struggle to make a decision as to which one is the best to get involved with. I have heard it said that several hundred MLMs start every month. Most of them will not survive two years, but new distributors don't know this until the company closes. Yes, I have been involved in companies that closed over the years. Most of them were very courteous, sent a letter informing distributors that they were stopping operations, did not bill again, and delivered all ordered products on time.

I thought that it would be a good idea to give new people to the industry a little history. Multi-level marketing is a much broader concept than its history, so this is by no means a complete story. I could probably write a book about my experience in the industry alone but this will give you a short version of how the industry reached this point.

Pyramid Scheme

A pyramid scheme is a type of scam which promises the investor that his initial investment will make them extraordinarily rich.

In reality, the pyramid scheme does not deliver on promised profits. In most cases, only the people who originate the pyramid scheme and a few of the initial salespeople or people who get in at the top of the pyramid will make any money. Most people merely lose money because their money only benefits those already involved in the scam. The pyramid scheme tends to manifest itself in products with exciting labels like "get rich quick," or "make millions without working." The hallmark of the pyramid scheme is that no actual product is offered. Instead, people pay a one-time fee to sign up to be part of the scheme, or they may purchase materials with instructions on how to sign up others. To make any money, the person must then sign up other people. Part of the revenue from new recruits is given to those who signed the person up for the program. These people in turn give part of their money to those who signed them up. Money flows upward toward the top of pyramid and the people who originated the pyramid scheme.

Another type of pyramid scheme is the chain letter requesting people to send money to the top name on a list of names. The person then crosses out the top name and forwards the letter on in the eventual hope that his or her name will eventually be at the top, at which time he will receive money. While this scheme promises to ultimately make one lots of money, it never works. Further, this chain letter pyramid scheme is illegal.

- ## Pyramid
- ## Ponzi Scheme

PONZI SCHEME

An investment swindle in which high profits are promised from fictitious sources and early investors are paid off with funds raised from later ones.

COMPENSATION PLANS

Stair step breakaway – This type of plan is characterized as having representatives who are responsible for both personal and group sales volumes. Volume is created by recruiting people and by retailing product. Various discounts or rebates may be paid to group leaders and a group leader can be any representative with one or more downline recruits. Once predefined personal and/or group volumes are achieved, a representative moves up a commission level. This continues until the representative's sales volume reaches the top

commission level and "breaks away" from their up-line. From that point on, the new group is no longer considered part of his up-line's group and the multi-level compensation aspect ceases. The original up-line usually continues to be compensated through override commissions and other incentives.

Uni-level – This type of plan is often considered the simplest of compensation plans. Uni-level plans pay commissions primarily based on the number of levels a recipient is from the original representative who is purchasing the product. Commissions are not based on title or rank achieved. By qualifying with a minimum sales requirement, representatives earn unlimited commissions on a limited number of levels of downline recruited representatives.

Matrix – This type of plan is similar to a uni-level plan, except limited numbers of representatives can be placed on the first level. Recruits beyond the maximum number of first level positions allowed are automatically placed in other downline (lower level) positions. Matrix plans often have a maximum width and depth. When all positions in a representa-

tive's downline matrix are filled (maximum width and depth is reached for all participants in a matrix), a new matrix may be started. Like uni-level plans, representatives in a matrix earn unlimited commissions on limited levels of volume with minimal sales quotas.

Binary – A binary plan is a multi-level marketing compensation plan which allows distributors to have only two front-line distributors. If a distributor sponsors more than two distributors, the excess are placed at levels below the sponsoring distributor's front-line. This "spillover" is one of the most attractive features to new distributors since they need to sponsor only two distributors to participate in the compensation plan. The primary limitation is that distributors must "balance" their two downline legs to receive commissions. Balancing legs typically requires that the number of sales from one downline leg constitute no more than a specified percentage of the distributor's total sales.

Hybrid – Hybrids are compensation plans constructed using elements of more than one type of compensation plan.

THINGS YOU DON'T NEED TO BE SUCCESSFUL IN NETWORK MARKETING

Credentials or degree – Thousands of people have been successful in networking without the benefit of college degrees and the like. Since networking is so unlike other businesses, the rules are different. An argument could almost be made against having diplomas in this business, for people may feel that because their sponsor has an advanced business degree they need one too. This is not re-creatable and entirely unnecessary. If you or your sponsor has a degree, great. It's just not necessary for success in network marketing.

Approval – Of anyone, except yourself. Sometimes even your spouse may not approve of your network marketing business. This is actually a frequent initial response, but we've seen thousands of people who have built huge businesses without the help of their spouse. Of course, after that, the spouse usually comes on board enthusiastically and things really takeoff. One of the hardest facts of business is that not everybody is ready for success or is as enlightened as you.

Don't be at all surprised to find that some of your closest friends and family members will ridicule you; not join your organization and or even listen to a presentation; question your sanity; ask why someone with a "real" job would "mess around with one of those multi-level deals"; or all of the above. Then they will feel obligated to regale you with horror stories of people who "got a horrible rash just drinking that stuff" or have "a garage full of that stuff they can't get rid of." It's best to give these "well-meaning" souls a wry smile, thank them for their input, and get away from them as quickly as possible.

Friends and Family in your network – Now please don't misunderstand, if you get them in your group, great! I know families with three generations in their networking business and it's a beautiful thing to behold. Other times, the hardest presentation you ever give might be to a family member or best friend. Sometimes you just can't be a prophet in your own hometown. Direct selling is full of individuals who have built networks in the thousands without having a single member of their family or so-called best friends, in their group. I know, because I'm one of them.

Cheap Advice – Oftentimes a new distributor will get involved with network marketing and get all kinds of well meaning advice from friends who have never built a networking business. If you want to know how to fly airplanes, you must get advice from an expert pilot. If you want to build a network, look at your sponsorship line and find someone who has already built a large network. Those are the people to seek out for advice.

Perfection – The perfect company, product line, or compensation plan hasn't been invented yet. Like everything in nature, it develops over time. Your job is to look at the whole picture, and if the pluses outweigh the minuses, get started. If you sit around waiting for perfection, you'll be waiting forever. Don't make the mistake many novices make which is to think that they can't do anything until they have tried every single product, read every scrap of literature, and completely understand every minute detail of the compensation plan. The important thing is to get started and learn as you go.

THREE THINGS YOU NEED TO BE SUCCESSFUL

Desire – A desire to really do this and get out of the "rat race" forever. If you really understand this business and have a true desire to help yourself and others, you're already 90 percent. Most people are happy with the way things are. People who desire better are the ones who change the world.

Enthusiasm – I can't begin to tell you how many times I have seen brand new distributors with no training, no experience, and no in-depth knowledge go out and build a network of twenty or thirty people their first month. They don't do this with skill, knowledge, or technique; they just muscle it through with sheer, unadulterated enthusiasm. Approach this adventure with the excitement it deserves; don't just attempt it — jump in, roll up your sleeves, make up your mind, and just do it!

Action – If you're waiting for the perfect plan — the perfect plan is to take action. You have to get started. Will you make mistakes? Of course! But, we're not brain surgeons here; nobody's going to die. Mistakes are part of the learning process and strengthen you for the long term. This booklet, the accompanying audiotape, and your sponsorship line will make sure you don't make any major mistakes which will harm your business. Relax and don't be afraid to move ahead. Knowledge without action is only a potential for power.

You've got the knowledge you need...

You've shown your wisdom by becoming a networker.

Now, let's get started!

Chapter Two

COMMIT TO OUR TRAINING SYSTEM

With Mega Success Secrets, our goal is to help you learn the ins and outs of operating a home-based business, especially in the network marketing industry.

With anything you are trying to accomplish, you must first understand the "HOW TOs." You would not try and become a doctor without completing medical school, would you? That is why it is so important to commit to a training program. With Mega Success Secrets we are not trying to replace your company's training program, since it is without doubt a good one; but we are here to enhance it. Many company training programs concentrate on specific areas, such as their product and or service, which is great, and you need to know these things. But you also need to know how to be successful in distributorship and recruiting.

In the network marketing industry, millions of dollars are made by recruiting distributors. Many leaders of these organizations create systems that seem to work for them, but may not necessarily work for you. The problem is not all systems can be duplicated, at least not to the newcomer.

If you commit to the Mega Success Secrets training program, we guarantee your success. Why do we feel so confident? It's because we have worked with the industry's best to create this book for you. So, no matter what company you represent or if you have not found a company yet, we will teach you the "INs and OUTs" of the industry.

COMPANY CONTACT INFORMATION

Why is this so important? When you start in a new business venture, you must have people you can go to for leadership, mentoring, coaching and just some basic questions. MLM is a communications business. Communicating with your team is equally important to communicating with your up-line leadership, starting with your sponsor.

Sponsor – This is the person who brought you into your business. He or she is the one who you are going to rely on to help get you started.

First up-line leader – This is the leader you fall under somewhere in their team. When someone becomes a front line or up-line leader, this means he has shown a commitment not only to being successful, but also to the company and their team. Some companies call the people directors, executives, regional managers or something similar. These leaders normally have a closer business relationship with the corporate office, which benefits all that are below them. If you have a problem getting in touché with your sponsor, the first up-line leader is the next person you should go to.

Corporate contact information – You need to know how to get in contact with the corporate office. Depending on the industry you are in, this can be of more importance. For instance, if you are in the travel industry and you are working on a big booking, you may need some advice or assistance from the corporate subject matter expert (SME). Many different systems are in place for this. Some companies have a phone tree directs you to the department you are looking for. Others have some kind of Help Desk Ticket submission system. Depending on the size of the company and staffing, those can be great tools or they can hinder your business. No matter what the system, you must understand how it works.

YOUR HOME PAGE

Normally, this is your product or service page. The page is provided by your company and is a one stop shop for everything, including your business opportunity. This has its benefits and its downfalls. Let's say you are in the business of health and nutrition, and you send a prospective customer to your site to view your products. The customer goes through the site, finds great prices and great product, and is ready to purchase. Then she sees an opportunity link, checks it out, and gets the impression that you are part of some fly-by-night company or a scam. So she doesn't buy, and you lose a customer. On the other hand, she may see the opportunity as a way to save even more money and possibly make some additional money. So as you see, pros and cons exist.

Know how your site is laid out and its contents. Nothing is more important than knowing your very own site and how to navigate around it. This site is what is supposed to help make you money. It is a tool. Know how your tools work.

YOUR MARKETING PAGE

Not all companies offer this but you want to make sure you have one. This page is where you share your opportunity with people. Remember you are in the people business. Like all network marketing companies, people offer the opportunity of distributorship. If you are not sure if your company offers a marketing page, then ask your sponsor.

Most marketing pages are set up to provide your prospect with all the information needed to make a sound decision. If your company does not have a marketing page and everything is part of your home page, you may inquire to see if they have an affiliation with a company that provides such a tool. Many third party companies handle all the marketing media. Normally, an outside company gives you access to numerous tools that you would normally not have.

Some of these tools are:

- Embedded videos
- Numerous lead capture pages
- Auto-responders
- Prospect tracking and more.

Once again, check with your sponsor or up-line leader to find out these details.

Domain Name

With most opportunities, you have two businesses. You have a product or service, and you have an opportunity. You want to separate the product from the opportunity by purchasing two individual internet domains. Remember, not everyone is going to join your team, but you have the opportunity to make everyone a customer of your product or service.

Decide on a domain name you like for your business. This is optional; however, it can be easier to find your website. Get your own domain name, such as www.yourbusinessname.com. When you join a company, you automatically get a domain name (http://www.Yourname.XYZbiz.com). Just try fitting that on a business card or expect people to remember it. Numerous companies on the web can provide domain services.

When you have your domains, it is important to have your business sites forwarded to your new domains. Due to the various companies that provide domain services, their set-up procedures may be slightly different. One setting you must ensure is not enabled is "Masking." We will not get into a technical explanation of what "Masking" does — just be sure it is not enabled.

BUSINESS CARDS

Create your own business cards. Some people like to learn about what product or service they have before sharing the business idea with others. However, you should let people know they can purchase products or services on your site. You are in XYZ business, so let people know you are in the business.

Check with your company. They may offer a service to provide you with business cards. Many companies offer a promotional media area where you can buy all kinds of promotional stuff to help you build your business. Business cards may be one of them. If you do not like the way the cards look, find out if you can get your own cards made. Many companies online have some great products and pricing.

We have found FL Print Services (a division of Faithful Life Publishers) to be a tremendous souce of quality business cards and promotional materials. These guys have great prices and the best customer service. All their work is done in the states and they ship all over the world. They offer a free online business card designer or you can have them design cards for you at a nominal fee.

http://bit.ly/p5SnA4

If you have decided to not only sell products or services but also offer the opportunity, which I highly recommend, purchase two sets of business cards. Not everyone is going to be interested in your opportunity. Have one card for your product or services and one for the opportunity.

SETTING UP YOUR OFFICE
(Use your own personal experiences)

- Filing System
- Computer & Software
- Index Cards
- Bank Accounts
- Day Planner
- Fax Machine
- Answering Machine

Chapter Three

STEPS TO SUCCESS

Set your goals — You must decide what you want to do with your networking business. Are you just interested in getting your products for free? Are you looking to make a few hundred dollars to cover your car payment? Or do you want to develop complete financial freedom? To reach your goals, you must first determine what they are then set a timetable to reach them.

Write down your goals — Goals are a dream with a deadline, so dreams must be written down. You also want to make sure they are specific and measurable. I believe the average person, following a system, can achieve financial independence in this business during a two to five year time period. Think about what you want to do right away; then think about what you'd like your two to five year plan to be.

Build dreams with your spouse and your sponsor. Reawaken those wants and desires you used to have but probably got lost somewhere along the way. Sometimes we get so busy in the bustle of everyday living that we lose sight of our dreams. It's important that you discover your "burn" — the burning desire that will keep you focused and motivated during the early development stages of your networking career.

SCHEDULE YOUR APPOINTMENT BOOK

- This business is built on your word and appointments. To build effectively, you must plan your work and schedule your time in the manner that best suits building your business.

• You're already using all 24 hours of every day already. To change your life and what you're getting out of it, you must change the way you're using your 24 hours. You must carve out at least seven to ten hours a week exclusively for building your business.

• Work closely with your sponsor to determine how to schedule your seven to ten hours for the first few weeks of your business.

Find out the dates of all upcoming functions for the next ninety days so you can schedule your work and other obligations around them. Also, learn the dates of any annual conventions and conferences. These are major events, critical to your success, and you want to make sure you're at these.

LEARN THE BASIC COMPANY PROCEDURES

To be independent, and proactively build your business, you must be able to operate without your sponsor's assistance for day-to-day minor things as soon as possible. Learn some of the basic company procedures as soon as you can including:

• How to order products
• How to fill out distributor applications, order forms and requests (Nowadays, mostly done online)
• How to transfer volume

Set aside a few hours quiet time (Sunday evenings are ideal for most people) to read your entire distributor kit. Learn which sections to go to for specific information and familiarize yourself with the forms. Study the rules and regulations and learn the code of ethics.

ORDER YOUR BUSINESS CARDS

Covered in chapter two, page 23.

COMPLETE YOUR PROSPECT LIST

Remember, don't talk to anyone about your business yet. Do that only after your sponsor directs you. For now, begin writing down the name and phone number of anyone you think of.

LEARN THE CORE QUALITIES OF A LEADER

Top networking leaders possess various key qualities. Some, or even many of these, you have already put into action. To be a leader and set an example that others can duplicate you must learn the remaining ones. To practice all nine core qualities means you've made and honored a commitment to "go core." To develop your business, you must identify and work with the people in your organization who are willing to make this same commitment. Let's take a look at these core qualities:

Use all of the products — To "go core" means that if your company has a product you would never buy a competing product for any reason. A "Brand X" product purchase takes money out of your business and puts it in someone else's. This kind of practice will put you out of business quickly. A core person never buys "Brand X," regardless of sales, convenience or any other reason. It's simply bad business. You must use all of your company's products that apply to you and be able to talk knowledgeably and enthusiastically about them to effectively build your business. Think of it this way — would you trust someone in the travel business who never took a vacation in his or her life?

Develop a consumer group — A great deal of sales will be to distributors who "buy from their own store" and use the products themselves. But many other people can benefit from your products or services and are not interested in building a business at this time. These people become your consumer group.

It's critical that you develop this consumer group. This is good business practice, because you service the people who aren't distributors; earn retail income; develop consistent income you can count on from regular customers; and, build personal group volume, which can keep you qualified to earn many other lucrative bonuses and incentives. It's a good goal when you're just starting out to develop a base of at least ten retail customers.

Make regular presentations — Like every business, network marketing requires consistently taking action steps. One of the most important of these is making regular presentations. Realistically, you need to be making one or two presentations a week when you start your business (working seven to ten hours a week). As your business grows, you will want to increase this number.

When you reach what I consider "full time" in this business (about 25 hours a week), you will want to be making three to five presentations a week. Of course, not all these presentations will be new prospects that you want to sponsor personally. Many of them will be presentations you are conducting for your people as you train them and build depth.

You must consistently make presentations in order to grow. Don't be misled into thinking you're growing your business with "busy work" (reading manuals, going to seminars, filling out forms, etc.). These things are important, but they are support functions to the real business which is making presentations to prospects.

Attend everything — Functions are the glue that holds your business together. Attending them helps you grow your business, gives you crucial training, and keeps you focused. In your regional area you will have the chance to attend opportunity showcases, product workshops and rallies. If these are two to three hours driving distance, you will want to attend. Other events, such as conventions and leadership conferences, are held annually. These are major, often life-changing events, and you'll want to schedule your vacation time around them so you never miss one.

Schedule time for personal development — If I've discovered one truth, it is this — your business will grow only as fast as you do. Initially, you need recruiting and training skills. Later, you need time management and organizational skills. Ultimately, however, you will need leadership, communication and empowerment abilities. To develop others, you must first develop yourself. It's important that you spend daily self-development time. For most people, this is best done in the morning, before you start your day. You might meditate, exercise, listen to inspirational tapes, or read anything that helps you grow your mind, body and soul. Set aside this time and stick to it.

Invest in audio recordings, books, and videos that help you develop. At every opportunity throughout the day, listen to recordings — when you're driving, walking, cycling, or have downtime. Also, don't end your day by watching the late news and then going to sleep. Make sure the last input you receive before going to bed is positive even if it's just reading one paragraph in an inspirational book. Many companies or sponsorship lines offer programs that provide positive inspirational material on a subscription basis. If you're in such a situation, you are quite fortunate, because much of the work of finding and getting good material is already done for you. Sign up right away and make sure your people do as well.

> NOTE: If your company doesn't have such a program, or you would like to supplement your program, I'd like to suggest that you consider a subscription to *The Brilliant Compensation*. http://www.brilliantcompensation.com

Be teachable — If you want to build your business in the fastest manner possible, you must be teachable and willing to be coached. You will find network marketing is quite different from traditional businesses. Things that work great in sales simply do not work well in network marketing. Your sponsorship line has learned the methods, strategies, and techniques that work best in your business. They will work with you and teach you everything they know without charging you a penny. Your sponsor is the repository of all the experience of many generations of distributors all the way to the company. Learn from them.

Be accountable — For years now, chain letters and money games have been masquerading as legitimate network marketing programs. This means those of us in true programs must be beyond reproach. We must set a standard of integrity much higher than the corporate world. Network marketing is a business of relationships, and relationships operate on trust. To earn and maintain that trust, you must be accountable. We can never tell a lie to our distributors or customers and be accountable. Accountability also means that when we write checks, they're good; when we promise to work with someone, we follow through; and when we commit to attend an event, we're on time.

Accountability means that when we have a product display with 24 products, there will still be 24 products on the table at the end of the night. It means never approaching someone else's prospect or attempting to steal distributors from another line.

You will create the culture of your organization. If you do it right it will mean you can hold a function and 800 women can leave their purses on their chairs, come back, and find everything exactly as they left it!
Edify the organization – Savvy distributors learn that they must edify their sponsorship line. When you point out the success and accomplishments of your sponsors, it makes those sponsors more effective when they come to work with both your prospects and distributors. Many times you will find it difficult to be a prophet in your hometown. Sometimes your friends and relatives aren't yet ready to accept that a powerful, positive concept can come from you. By edifying your sponsorship line and then bringing your prospects to them, you'll have support to hold you over until you develop some initial success and credibility. Likewise, your sponsorship line can help you when you're working with your new distributors.

Follow the system — Leaders understand that "lone rangers" can be successful initially, but will not enjoy long term success.

For residual income and walk-way security, you must follow a step-by-step re-creatable system meaning everyone in your organization uses the same pre-approach pack, the same company materials pack, employs the same training procedures, and follows a standardized presentation. This way, the method you use to bring in new people is the same method they use to bring in their new people. The method can be duplicated. Regardless of someone's previous job experience, their education level or confidence level, they can do the business exactly the same way you did.

Your sponsorship line has learned what works and what doesn't. They have created the system based upon that experience.

Follow the system and you have the resources of the entire sponsorship line working for you. If you change the system, you lose the benefits of having all those resources at your disposal. Also, when you change the system by substituting a different tape or modifying the presentation, etc., you send a message to your people that it's okay to change the system.

What happens if the first level people change the system just a little, and then the next level changes the system a little bit, and the changes continue down through the group? By the third level, no system exists, so you have no security and no potential for walk-away, residual income. Always follow the system!

Schedule your first presentation — It's very possible that your sponsor may offer to conduct a home meeting for you to make the presentations to your initial prospects. Or they may be conducting hotel meetings that you can bring your people to. They may also help you with 2-on-1 presentations with some of your people. Schedule your first couple of weeks' presentations with your sponsor and write them in your planner.

> Note: In cases of rapid organizational grow your sponsor may not yet be qualified to make a presentation. If so, it is okay to go further up the sponsorship line and find someone to help you.

This is a critical part of your training. As you watch and listen to your sponsorship line make your initial presentations (taking good notes, I hope), you will be learning how it's done. The sooner you learn to conduct a presentation yourself, the sooner you're on your way to independence.

You can then duplicate this process with your people. By following this system, you will be building secure lines with the potential for walk-away, residual income.

Place your first order — You must use the products or services personally so you can get excited about them. How much should you order? Somewhere between what you need and where you're nervous. I say this only halfway in jest. You see, we've found that "just what you need" is not enough. You'll need some inventory for reselling to new distributors plus samples for temporarily out-of-stock items and personal marketing. You certainly don't want to have a garage or warehouse full of product. But do make sure you have enough products on hand to build your business.

Educate yourself!

What is your why?

This is the MOST POWERFUL STEP you'll take. It is what will "start" your business, and more importantly, it is what "sustains" your business. "What is your why?" is a question that you should always ask yourself.

- Why did you join the company that you did?
- What is your main motivation?
    - A new house
    - College for you or the kids
    - New car
    - Time freedom

- Financial freedom
- This is defined by you!

• What do you hope to accomplish?

• Identify each of your TOP 3...
- Immediate Desires
- Long Term Goals
- Awesome Dreams

Goals don't work unless YOU DO!

Find and fully know your "WHY"! That is the reason you are in your own business. Is it to be able to stay at home and raise your children while still earning a good income? Maybe it is to be your own boss or gain more time and financial freedom. Whatever it is, make a list on a piece of paper and post it on your refrigerator. Look at it several times daily. Begin to think and believe you have already accomplished these goals! In a short time you will begin to feel change of ATTITUDE coming over you.

Time management — Personal time management skills are essential skills for effective people. People who use these techniques routinely are the highest achievers in all walks of life, from business to sports to public service. If you use these skills well, then you will be able to function exceptionally well, even under intense pressure. What's more, as you master these skills, you'll find that you take control of your workload and say goodbye to the often intense stress of work overload.

The 80:20 rule – This rule is neatly summed up in the Pareto Principle, which says that typically 80 percent of unfocused effort generates only 20 percent of results. This means that the remaining 80 percent of results are achieved with only 20 percent of the effort. While the ratio is not always 80:20, this broad pattern of a small proportion of activity generating, non-scalar returns recurs so frequently that it is the norm in many situations.

By applying the time management tips and skills in the next section you can optimize your effort to ensure that you concentrate as much of your time and energy as possible on the high payoff tasks. You can achieve the greatest benefit possible with the limited amount of time available to you.

Time management tools – In this section, we start off with simple and practical techniques, so that you can get off to a quick start in taking control of your time. The e-book on *Beating Procrastination and Activity Logs* will help you quickly eliminate the most common time wasters, while the e-books on *Action Plans* and *Prioritized To Do Lists* teach simple techniques helping you focus on the most important short-term activities.

- E-books to aid you in time management
    - *How Good is Your Time Management?*
    - *Beating Procrastination*
    - *Activity Logs*
    - *Prioritized To Do Lists*
    - *Personal Goal Setting*
    - *Effective Scheduling*

• Attending your company's next big event – Big events (conventions, regionals, and Super Saturdays) are the VERY HEART of a successful business. The more people you have at an event has a direct effect on the "BIGNESS" and "STABILITY" of your business. It's no wonder that it's ESSENTIAL to attend ALL big events. During these events, you have key leaders in the company delivering the opportunity, conducting training, and sharing changes coming down the road. I cannot stress how important it is to attend these events. The best part of these events is that you meet so many other people in your company. It allows you to build friendships and business relationships that can last a lifetime.

• Attend local events – Meetings are a very important part of your business. A meeting's primary purpose is to help you stay excited, motivated, and rejuvenated. Meetings are also used to help share the business opportunity to YOUR guests. Think of your local meetings as practice for the "BIG EVENTS." Meetings make money, which means the more you and your team attend, the stronger and larger your team becomes. If you have problems attending opportunity meetings, plan a gathering at your home (Product or Opportunity Party). Tell your friends, family, and co-workers that you are planning a small gathering to celebrate your new promotion. Let your guests know you will have food, beverages, and fun. Tell them you are so excited and will tell them more at the gathering. (At the gathering show your company presentation and then you can watch your checks grow).

Chapter Four

GOLDEN RULES OF GOAL SETTING

Have you thought about what you want to be doing in five years' time?... Are you clear about what your main objective at work is at the moment?... Do you know what you want to have achieved by the end of today?

If you want to succeed, you need to set goals. Without goals, you lack focus and direction. Goal setting not only allows you to take control of your life's direction, but also provides you a benchmark for determining whether you are actually succeeding. Think about it — having a million dollars in the bank is only proof of success if one of your goals is to amass riches. If your goal is to practice acts of charity, then keeping the money for yourself is suddenly contrary to how you would define success.

To accomplish your goals, however, you need to know how to set them. You can't simply say, "I want," and expect it to happen. Goal setting is a process that starts with careful consideration of what you want to achieve and ends with a lot of hard work to actually do it. In between some very well-defined steps transcend the specifics of each goal. Knowing these steps will allow you to formulate goals that you can accomplish. Here are our Five Golden Rules of Goal Setting:

RULE #1: SET GOALS THAT MOTIVATE YOU

When you set goals for yourself, it is important that they motivate you. Make sure your goal is something that's important to you and has value in achieving it. If you have little interest in the outcome, or it is irrelevant given the larger picture, then the chances of you putting in the work to make it happen are slim. Motivation is key to achieving goals.

Set goals that relate to the high priorities in your life. Without this type of focus you can end up with far too many goals, leaving you too little time to devote to each one. Goal achievement requires commitment, so to maximize the likelihood of success, you need to feel a sense of urgency and have an "I must do this" attitude. When you don't have this "must do" factor, you risk putting off what you need to do to make the goal a reality and end up feeling disappointed and frustrated with yourself, both of which are de-motivating.

You can end up in a very destructive "I can't do anything or be successful at anything" frame of mind.

Tip: To make sure your goal is motivating, write down why it's valuable and important to you. Ask yourself, "If I were to share my goal with others, how would I tell them to convince them it was a worthwhile goal?" You can use this motivating value statement to help you if you start to doubt yourself or lose confidence in your ability to actually make it happen.

Rule #2: Set SMART goals

You have probably heard of "SMART goals" already. But do you always apply the rule? The simple fact is that for any goal to be achieved it must be designed to be SMART. Many variations on what SMART stands for are out there, but the essence is this… Goals should be:

- Specific
- Measurable
- Attainable
- Relevant
- Time Bound

Set specific goals – Your goal must be clear and well defined. Vague or generalized goals are not achievable because they don't provide sufficient direction. Remember, you need goals to show you the way. How useful would a map of the United States be if there were only state borders marked on it and you were trying to get from Miami to Los Angeles? Do you even know which state you are starting from let alone which one you're headed to? Make it as easy as you can to get where you want to go by defining precisely where it is you want to end up.

Set measurable goals – Include precise amounts, dates, etc., in your goals so you can measure your degree of success. If your goal is simply defined as "to reduce expenses," how will you know when you are successful? Is success if you have a 1 percent reduction in one month's time or in two year's time when you have a 10 percent reduction? Without a way to measure your success, you miss out on the celebration that comes with knowing you actually achieved something.

Set attainable goals – Make sure that it's possible to achieve the goals you set. If you set a goal that you have no hope of achieving, you will only demoralize yourself and erode your confidence. However, resist the urge to set goals that are too easy. Accomplishing a goal that you didn't have to work very hard for can be an anticlimax and can make you fear setting future goals that carry a risk of non-achievement. By setting realistic yet challenging goals, you hit the balance you need. These are the types of goals that require you to "raise the bar" and they bring the greatest personal satisfaction.

Set relevant goals – Goals should be relevant to the direction you want your life and career to take. By keeping goals aligned, you'll develop the focus you need to get ahead and do what you want. Set widely scattered and inconsistent goals and you'll fritter your time - and your life - away.

Set time-bound goals – You goals must have a deadline. This again, is so that you know when to celebrate your success. When you are working on a deadline, your sense of urgency increases and achievement will come that much quicker.

RULE #3: SET GOALS IN WRITING

The physical act of writing down a goal makes it real and tangible. You have no excuse for forgetting about it. As you write, use the word "will" instead of "would like to" or "might." For example, "I will reduce my operating expenses by 10 percent this year." Not, "I would like to reduce my operating expenses by 10 percent this year." The first goal statement has power and you can "see" yourself reducing expenses; the second lacks passion and gives you an out if you get sidetracked.

> Tip 1: Frame your goal statement positively. If you want to improve your retention rates say, "I will hold on to all existing employees for the next quarter" rather than "I will reduce employee turnover." The first one is motivating; the second one still has a get-out clause "allowing" you to succeed even if some employees leave.

> Tip 2: If you use a "to do" list, make yourself a "to do" list template that has your goals at the top of it.

Post your goals in visible places to remind yourself every day of what it is you intend to do. Put them on your walls, desk, computer monitor, bathroom mirror or refrigerator as a constant reminder. You can even post them in the *Mind Tools Career Excellence Club* forum and share them with other members for added motivation.

http://www.mindtools.com

RULE #4: MAKE AN ACTION PLAN

This step is often missed in the process of goal setting. You get so focused on the outcome that you forget to plan all of the steps that are needed along the way. By writing out the individual steps, and then crossing each one off as you complete it, you'll realize that you are making progress towards your ultimate goal. If your goal is big and demanding or long-term, setting an action plan is especially important. Read our article on "Action Plans" for more on how to do this.

RULE #5: STICK WITH IT!

Remember, goal setting is an ongoing activity, not just a means to an end. Build in reminders to keep you on track and remember to review your goals continuously. Your end destination may remain quite similar over the long term but the action plan you set for yourself along the way can change significantly. Make sure the relevance, value, and necessity remain high.

KEY POINTS

Goal setting is much more than simply saying you want something to happen. Unless you clearly define exactly what you want and understand why you want it in the first place, your odds of success are considerably reduced. By following the Five Golden Rules of Goal Setting you can set goals with confidence and enjoy the satisfaction that comes along with knowing you achieved what you set out to do. What will you decide to accomplish today?

Three basic types of goals

Improvement goals – Things that we want to change or make better, such as losing weight, quitting smoking, or having better relationships.

Achievement goals – Things that we want to accomplish, such as top salesperson, greatest golfer, or best teacher.

Financial goals – Things that we want to acquire, like making a million dollars, being financially independent, owning cars, homes, etc.

Ask a majority of people about their goals, and they will typically give some vague, general answer. If it's an improvement goal, they may tell you that they want to lose weight. While they may be able to lose weight without a clearly defined goal, their chances of really succeeding long-term are slim until they specify how much weight they want to lose and devise a plan for how they are going to do it. If you don't know where you're going, how will you know when you get there?

Three types of time-driven goals

Long-term goals – These relate to the next few years. In college, long-term goals might include things like graduating on the dean's list or with honors, running for student government, obtaining an internship or specific type of employment experience while in school, or preparing for a specific job when you finish college.

Short-term goals – These relate to the current term. What can you accomplish this semester, or even quarter, that will move you towards your long-term goals? Short-term goals might include passing classes, getting good grades, creating a study group for a specific course, or completing and turning in all assignments on time.

Immediate goals – These are the steps that need to be taken to successfully complete each short-term goal. Note that they always relate to a larger goal. Each short-term goal can be broken down into a plan to meet that goal. For example, if a short-term goal is to pass courses, immediate goals might include attending all classes, doing all assignments on time, and studying for exams.

SEVEN STEPS TO SET BUSINESS GOALS YOU WILL ACHIEVE

Step One: Begin with the end in mind – Work backwards. Decide where you want to be at the end of the year. With that in mind, where will you need to be six months and three months from now? For instance, in your business, you might set goals for revenue or for the number of new clients or projects completed. Next, break it down to what you will need to achieve in the next 30 days.

Step Two: Passion will provide the motivation you need – If you're passionate about the outcome, your chances of success will multiply. When we want something enough, the end result seems worth all the effort to get there — we're much more willing to pay the price. List all the benefits to you for reaching a goal. You'll also be more likely to achieve goals based on your own core values.

Step Three: Commit your goals to paper – Writing out your goals and displaying them where you see them often will increase your chances of reaching them. Word them carefully and be specific. Create an action plan with due dates and clear action steps for each goal. Prioritizing your goals will help when life gets busy. Then, set a timeline to get yourself going.

Step Four: Test your goals – Make sure your goals are realistic — a bit of a stretch but still within reach. Setting idealistic goals that are too difficult to achieve, or having too many goals, can lead to defeat and discouragement. Make sure each goal is measurable — you need to know if you've won or lost. Be flexible. When a goal isn't working, find out why. If circumstances change, a goal may no longer be useful. Give yourself permission to modify or even abandon a goal altogether.

Step Five: You'll need accountability and support along the way – Find an accountability buddy who'll hold your feet to the fire. It's amazing how motivated we can be to complete a project when we have to answer to someone else.

Step Six: Keep moving forward – Review goals and gauge your progress regularly. Make this part of your daily or weekly planning process. Do something every day, no matter how small, that will take you closer to your desired result. Keep steadily plodding forward. This may not seem exciting, but looking back occasionally to see how far you've come will prove very rewarding.

Encourage yourself with positive self-talk. Silence your "inner critic" — allow no negative internal dialogue about the process or your ability to achieve a goal.

Employ all your senses to keep you on track. Ask yourself how it will feel when you achieve your goal. Think about it. Imagine it.

Use the power of pictures. What will it look like when you achieve a goal? Post pictures where you'll see them daily. Divorce coach Laurie Cameron always wanted to own a convertible, so she cut out a picture and put it up in her office. It happened to be a gold 2000 Chrysler Sebring convertible. After looking at the picture for a couple of years, wishing she could afford it, she declared out loud that her next car would be a convertible! She called an auto broker, told him she wanted a convertible and that she wasn't in a hurry — next week or next year, it didn't matter. Three days later, he called back. He'd found a car at an auction and asked if she was interested. It was gold 2000 Chrysler Sebring that she has thoroughly enjoyed driving since!

Step Seven: Enjoy the journey – Reward yourself along the way for small accomplishments. Celebrate achievements — this could be a dinner out at a favorite restaurant, an ice cream cone, time out to visit with an old friend over a latte at the local coffee shop or a walk in the park. Each day, do something you love to do.

We suggest you set goals in all areas of your life: family, relationships, finances, spiritual, physical, educational and cultural — not just business. This will lead to a more balanced life.

You may not make great strides overnight, but like the tortoise, if you faithfully continue to make steady progress, you will reach your goals.

Chapter Five

10 SPONSORING TIPS TO FOLLOW BEFORE MAKING CALLS

1. Make the prospect comfortable – You must make the prospect comfortable quickly, and keep him in a comfortable state of mind. How do you do that? Simple. You must be comfortable with what you are doing, showing no pressure at all in your conversation, and staying warm and friendly. Keep talking about the prospect, what interests him and what he is looking for. People are comfortable talking about what interests them, not you.

2. Keep the conversation focused on the prospect – The prospect is listening to a particular radio station KIA-AM. It is a VERY important radio station to the prospect. It is radio "Keep It All About Me." You must keep the network marketing conversation focused on what he wants to see happen in his life and his future. Focus on him and him only, and continue to ask questions and keep a "TINY" focus — Their Interests Not Yours! It's ALL about the prospect. Keep your focus on him.

3. Build Trust – If the prospect does not trust you, you will not sponsor him. You must get him to trust you, as this is one of the cornerstones of sponsoring. Come across as "agenda-less" and with no motives, except to see if your business is something they would want to explore.

Operate in total Integrity. If you don't, it will catch up with you. Keep the prospect's life in focus, not your life. If you do, your business will become a greater focus to the prospect.

4. Listen to the Prospect; Don't Just Hear – Many people hear a prospect, but few listen to the prospect. The prospect will tell you all you need to know to close. Hearing is processing only the words, not the meaning and emotions.

Most people are too busy thinking about what they are going to say next, rather than listening to the prospect. Good hearing includes phrases like "Would you please tell me what you meant by that?"; "That was interesting"; or "Tell me what you are really looking for in life." Those who hear with the ears have shallow hearing, while those that listen with the heart and to the emotions have success listening and actually hear the prospect with a depth that is magnetic to success.

5. Take the pressure off the prospect – So many folks in the industry have a tendency to put some form of pressure on the prospect thinking that will help motivate him. It doesn't. Pressure is a sure way of pushing the prospect away and making their defenses go up. Take the pressure off with a pressure relief phrase, like "I am not sure this is something that is right for you" or "I am not sure this would be a fit for you." These phrases simply take the pressure off and show the prospect that you only want what is best for him and his family.

6. Connect with the prospect and they must connect with you – Connection is the secret to getting the prospect moving toward your psychologically. It is the process of asking questions and finding things that you have in common, you can relate to, you can share, you both agree with, etc. The more that a prospect feels connected to you, the more that your sponsoring magnetism is growing. Connecting phrases for sponsoring include ones like "You and I have some things in common"; "I can relate to that!"; or "I totally agree with you." People listen closely to people they feel connected with because they feel comfortable with those people.

7. Paint word pictures in full color. We think in pictures – When you think, you actually see an image in your mind, and that picture becomes a thought. Your prospect thinks that way too. If you are giving him only details and facts, then you are not going to set his dreams in motion.

You must paint him there in his dream on the canvass of his mind. Your words are the brush strokes, and your emotions are the color. Imagine the feeling of: "Can you see yourself...?"; "How would your family enjoy the results if you really achieved...?"; or "I can see you living in that home, can't you?" Find out what the prospect wants to happen in his life that is not happening, and then paint him there in his mind.

8. Have something for the prospect; do not want something from the prospect – Many times, we come to the prospect, and we have a dollar bill stuck to our foreheads. The prospect can feel this very quickly. You must not approach a prospect with your hand out mentally empty, as if asking for a crumb of bread. You never want to shake someone's hand and have him feel like a fifty dollar bill. You must have your hand out filled with hope, dreams, success, fulfillment, and an incredible lifestyle, ready to give those to the prospect. If you do, you will have a radically different mindset. One is a "taking" mindset, and the other is a "giving" mindset. The prospect will ALWAYS be drawn towards a GIVING mindset, not a TAKING one. Have the gift of success ready to give your prospect, not the desire to take something from him. In sponsoring, you always have more power than from just you.

9. Pour out hope, not hype – Pouring out is an art that successful people and leaders have mastered. It is simply taking the best of your emotions, and pouring them into a person with your words, caring and belief. Hope is the master product in network marketing. Many people are so focused on getting their prospect excited, they forget that hope is more powerful than hype. Hype comes from the head, and hope comes from the heart. One is heard, and the other is felt. Pour out with your words and emotions the power of hope for a better future, income, and life style. As you pour in, the prospect will begin to pour out his heart, and you will know the truth of what he is hoping for in life.

10. Do not be emotionally attached to the result – So many times, we get discouraged and down when results of our recruiting efforts do not align with what we want to happen. Our emotions kick in, we start doubting ourselves and what we are doing, and fear of failure starts to creep in. Then you get so discouraged, and you end up giving up, the result of your emotions controlling you, not you controlling your emotions.

You must step back from results, as you must understand that many people are too busy living their lives to ever put more life in their living. Timing might not be right. They may be totally happy where they are in life. They are not saying no to you, but to themselves. Don't get emotionally attached to the possibility of your prospect enrolling until he has given you a reason to.

Discouragement is a result of your emotions dominating reality, but reality is more people than you can imagine are out in the world looking for you. Go talk to them, and bless them with your business, instead of being bound and imprisoned by chains of negative emotion in network marketing.

THE IMPORTANCE OF POSTURING

Here are concepts to apply for success:

Posture is an attitude – Coming across with posture really boils down to positive self-esteem and a strong belief in your opportunity and product. Posture is a conviction you have in your voice and a persona about where you're going, the company/product you represent, and what kind of potential is available to you and others. That's it in a nutshell. People may not flock to you or buy your product or join your sales organization (team) simply because you asked them to. As a matter of fact, they probably won't if you simply share your product and opportunity but display no posture.

Building a productive team of producers is about looking for people to partner with and develop as leaders, not simply signing people up. The key to finding these potential leaders is in the interview process. Professional networkers sort for quality people; they don't "sell" people on the opportunity or products.

Perception is reality – People want to be associated with someone who is busy and successful. When you spend a lot of time (hours) with one prospect or potential team member, you don't come across as a successful entrepreneur. Instead, you appear as a desperate sales person.

Lead! Don't follow. You're the leader of your own home-based enterprise. When you prospect, behave as a leader should behave.

Don't allow your prospect to take control of the conversation, behave rudely, and make you jump through hoops to convince him to join your business.

Remember this is your own business and you are sorting for potential partners. Anyone who behaves rudely or is obnoxious would likely not be a good partner anyway. Let them go...NEXT.

When you take your home-based opportunity seriously and treat it with the time and respect it deserves, others will do the same. You literally have your hands on a multi-million dollar opportunity so be sure you are treating it that way. Your confidence or lack of confidence many times will be the determining factor in your prospect making the decision to either buy your product or get started in your business. Prospects enroll in a home-based business opportunity with the person they perceive to be a leader, and they buy products they perceive to be of value.

No need to make this more difficult than it really is. It's simply business (that doesn't mean always easy), however it requires a couple of things from you:

- A willingness to get out of your comfort zone.
- Action! Action! Action!
- Leads! Leads! Leads!
- Prospects! Prospects! Prospects!

Even if you are completely scared to death and you stutter a lot, you can still sponsor and sell services by simply being able to talk to a lot of people. You learn by doing. You get good by practicing. A "no" answer means the timing isn't right for your prospect or they're not ready to get involved in something at this time. It is not personal and you must be willing to move on to the "next" person. Find the yes's!

Prospecting with posture is caring enough about your fellow human being to not be intimidated when asking someone how much money he really believes he deserves to earn and how freely he deserves it. It's taking the bull by the horns, taking a stand about your future and inviting as many quality people as possible to join you in your quest for success. It's recognizing that not everybody is going to want to step out of his comfort zone and make the trip, and it's about being okay with his or her decision.

IDENTIFYING AND UNDERSTANDING YOUR TARGET MARKET

Network marketing is no different than any other business. In order to succeed it is essential to understand your target market.

Promoting your opportunity to the wrong audience will drain your cash flow and eventually force you out of business. But it is amazing how many network marketers are unaware of this basic marketing principle. So many up-line leaders teach the "shot gun" approach of making your list, getting information to the people, and seeing who sticks. The shot gun approach is one of the reasons we have a 95% failure rate in this industry. The bottom line is that any network marketer really needs to learn the basics of target marketing in order to succeed in the business.

Before we go on, it should be stated that nothing is wrong with mailing out some product CDs to your warm market. It's what you want to do, but that's just your first step, not your only step. There are smarter ways to build your business.

Define your target market – These are people who are ALREADY actively using or consuming what you are promoting. The first rule of marketing is to sell products people want to buy, to the people who want to buy them. You can't sell a steak to a vegetarian. You can't market a product to someone who does not have the desire to consume it. You can't sell an opportunity to someone who isn't looking for one, no matter how "perfect" you think he would be or how much money you think he could make.

In this industry, you have two target markets:

1) Potential business partners. This target market consists of one primary group of people - other network marketers, or people who buy products and services related to building a network marketing business.

Network marketers are opportunity buyers, meaning they are actively buying what you sell. They understand the network marketing industry so you don't have to spend time explaining basic concepts and the business model. They are also experienced enough to know that it takes work and application to build a successful network marketing business.

It is essential to make the distinction between "opportunity buyers" and "opportunity seekers."

An *opportunity seeker* is anyone looking for a quick fix to their current problem — nothing more than someone who filled out a survey and raised his hand to say "I would like to earn extra money." Specific ways of marketing to opportunity seekers exist but don't be lulled into thinking that this is your prime market for business partners.

Target *opportunity buyers* for the greatest chance of success.

2) Our product customers. Let's use a nutrition-based opportunity as an example. Most people would think that their target market consists of people who have health issues, which is true to a point. But we can get, and want to get, more specific than that. How about people who have health concerns and who actually spend money each month on health products? These people are your TRUE target market. So how do you find people these people? People who have acid reflux, for example, currently buy prescription medication for it and are between the ages of thirty and sixty. If you have a nutrition product that helps relieve acid reflux, then those are the specific people you want to market to, not your Uncle Bob, unless, of course, he has acid reflux. Just remember the difference between people who simply inquire about your offer and those who are already spending money on something similar.

"Target marketing" is the foundation of your marketing efforts. Clearly identifying your target market is a major step to achieving success in any business. Network marketing is no exception.

Chapter Six

EFFECTIVE COMMUNICATIONS

Effective communication is all about clearly conveying your messages to other people. It's also about receiving information that others are sending to you, with as little distortion as possible.

Effective communication involves effort from both the sender of the message and the receiver. And it's a process that can be fraught with error, with messages muddled by the sender or misinterpreted by the recipient. When this isn't detected, it can cause tremendous confusion, wasted effort, and missed opportunity. In fact, communication is only successful when both the sender and the receiver understand the same information as a result of the communication.

By successfully getting your message across, you convey your thoughts and ideas effectively. When not successful, the thoughts and ideas that you actually send do not necessarily reflect what you think, causing a communications breakdown and creating roadblocks that stand in the way of your goals — both personally and professionally.

In a recent survey of recruiters from companies with more than 50,000 employees, communication skills were cited as the single most important factor in choosing managers. The survey, conducted by the University of Pittsburgh's Katz Business School, points out that communication skills, including written and oral presentations, as well as an ability to work with others, are the main factors contributing to job success.

In spite of the increasing importance placed on communication skills, many individuals continue to struggle, unable to communicate their thoughts and ideas effectively — whether in verbal or written format. This inability makes it nearly impossible for them to compete effectively in the workplace and stands in the way of career progression.

Being able to communicate effectively is, fore, essential if you want to build a successful career. To do this, you must understand what your message is, what audience you are sending it to, and how it will be perceived. You must also weigh-in the circumstances surrounding your communications, such as situational and cultural context.

THE IMPORTANCE OF REMOVING BARRIERS

Problems with communication can pop up at every stage of the communication process (which consists of the sender, encoding, the channel, decoding, the receiver, feedback and the context – see the points below). At each stage, the potential for misunderstanding and confusion is there.

To be an effective communicator and to get your point across without misunderstanding and confusion, your goal should be to lessen the frequency of problems at each stage of the process with clear, concise, accurate, well-planned communications. We follow the process through below, step-by-step.

> **Source** – As the source of the message, you need to be clear about why you're communicating, and what you want to communicate. You also need to be confident that the information you're communicating is useful and accurate.

> **Message** – The message is the information that you want to communicate.

> **Encoding** – This is the process of transferring the information you want to communicate into a form that can be sent and correctly decoded at the other end. Your success in encoding depends partly

on your ability to convey information clearly and simply, but also on your ability to anticipate and eliminate sources of confusion (for example, cultural issues, mistaken assumptions, and missing information.) A key part of this is knowing your audience. Failure to understand who you are communicating with will result in delivering messages that are misunderstood.

Channel – Messages are conveyed through channels. Verbal channels include face-to-face meetings, telephone, and video-conferencing. Written channels include letters, e-mails, memos and reports. Different channels have different strengths and weaknesses. For example, it's not particularly effective to give a long list of directions verbally, while you'll quickly cause problems if you give someone negative feedback using email.

Decoding – Just as successful encoding is a skill, so is successful decoding (for example, taking the time to read a message carefully or listen actively to it.) Just as confusion can arise from errors in encoding, it can also arise from decoding errors. Confusion is particularly the case if the decoder doesn't have enough knowledge to understand the message.

Receiver – Your message is delivered to individual members of your audience. No doubt you have in mind the actions or reactions you hope your message will get from this audience. Keep in mind, though, that each of these individuals enters into the communication process with ideas and feelings that will undoubtedly influence his understanding of your message and his response. To be a successful communicator, you should consider these ideas and feelings before delivering your message, and act appropriately.

Feedback – Your audience will provide you with feedback, as verbal and nonverbal reactions to your communicated message. Pay close attention to this feedback, since it is the only thing able to give you confidence that your audience has understood your message. If you find a misunderstanding, at least you have the opportunity to send the message a second time.

Context – The situation in which your message is delivered is the context, including the surrounding environment or broader culture (corporate culture, international cultures, and so on).

REMOVING BARRIERS AT ALL THESE STAGES

To deliver your messages effectively, you must commit to breaking down the barriers that exist within each of the stages of the communication process.

Let's begin with the message itself. If your message is too lengthy, disorganized, or contains errors, you can expect the message to be misunderstood and misinterpreted. Use of poor verbal skills and body language can also confuse the message. Barriers in context tend to stem from senders offering too much information too fast. When in doubt here, less is oftentimes more. It is best to be mindful of the demands on other people's time, especially in today's ultra-busy society.

Once you understand barriers, you need to work to understand your audience's culture, making sure you can converse and deliver your message to people of different backgrounds and cultures within your own organization, in your country and even abroad.

QUALITIES/ATTRIBUTES OF A GOOD COMMUNICATOR

Be interested in the prospect – Show general interest. Make the prospect feel that you are truly interested in him and that you are really paying attention. You want to be interested in him, not interesting. If he senses you are sincerely interested in him, he will have an easier time opening up to you. If he has any experience in network marketing, he will share that with you.

If you find a company that you both had in common, listen to his experience. Let him share successes and failures. Do not begin to share yours; if you do, you take the focus off the prospect and put it on you. Now you are just trying to be interesting.

Do not be distracted by anything – Experts tell us that it's not what you say but how you say it. Well, just where do you learn how to do that?

When talking with your prospect, after the first silent statement of "I'm interested in you," the next thing you do is "DON'T BE DISTRACTED BY ANYTHING."

When you are distracted by something, immediately your silent statement of "I'm interested in you" is gone because you're not interested in the prospect if you're distracted by something else. Instead, you're interested in the email that just came in or the waiter that just stepped up to the table.

While talking with your prospect, don't take your attention off the prospect until the prospect's attention goes off you. If the prospect looks at a TV, a waiter, a child, etc., don't keep staring at him. Shift your focus to what he's looking at. When you're on the phone, keep focused on the conversation — no multitasking! Here's a valuable MLM training tip to make note of: Extremely important things get skipped while you're multitasking. Your replies to the prospect's statements and questions will often be incorrect, inappropriate, or not timed correctly. And don't think for a second that the prospect doesn't notice. It may be "okay" with him, but he knows he is second place (at least) in your order of importance. This is never okay.

When you're at a business meeting with your guest, don't be distracted by the environment. When someone arrives late to the meeting don't look at the late person. I don't care if EVERYONE looks — don't look. Keep your eyes on the presenter; this reveals the importance you place on the content of the speaker's message. Your guest will notice your actions. The same is true for someone leaving the room — don't look.

Often MLM training meetings are more relaxed, but the same rule applies — don't be distracted by anything in the environment. Here is a list of some common things I see people distracted by:

- Men distracted by a cute girl walking by.
- Women noticing the wardrobe of another woman walking by.
- Television that's in the room.
- Children or pets at an in-home meeting.
- Cell phones ringing.
- Someone more interesting than the prospect - which should NEVER be the case.
- The rattling of a health/candy bar or a piece of candy.

<u>Forget everything else and just pay attention to your prospect.</u>

Have a sincere friendly facial expression – Successful communication with MLM business prospects is more than just what you say. Ever wonder what you look like from someone else's perspective? It really is an interesting thing to ponder. Next time you are just in a casual conversation with your spouse or friend, have him or her put a mirror in front of you sometime during your conversation.

The very second you see yourself in the mirror, I bet you CHANGE YOUR FACIAL EXPRESSION. What would you change it to? The way you think you look to everyone. Very often how you look versus how everyone thinks you look is very different.

If you're one of those who love to people-watch, the funniest people-watching situation is when you can sit near a mirror and watch people look at themselves. It certainly would have made a great Candid Camera skit.

If you are truly interested in your prospect and you're not distracted by anything in the environment (this also includes not being distracted by what's going on INSIDE OF YOU), you can't help but have a sincere friendly facial expression. Of course, as your prospect talks, your facial expression will change slightly based on what they're telling you, but it will always revert back to SINCERE and FRIENDLY.

What stops a person from having this desired facial expression? The number one reason is fear. As the distributor is talking with his prospect, the distributor is fearful of how the prospect will react to the business, so his face (if he looks in a mirror) has the look of fear or concern. This concerned or worried look is describing what is going on in the distributor's head! Your facial expression expresses what you're thinking.

The second thing that stops a person from having this desired facial expression is that he's been given some lame advice about mirroring and matching every move his prospect makes. Other bad advice is that you should always maintain eye contact, taking this to an extreme, and ending up boring holes through your prospect which intimidates the prospect.

Just be comfortable with your prospect and maintain comfortable eye contact with a sincere, friendly facial expression.

And I should add that you should keep a friendly facial expression even when you're on the phone, calling prospects. Even though they can't see you, your expression carries through your voice and the words you say. So when you're talking with prospects, keep this MLM training tip in the forefront of your mind.

Just be comfortable with your prospect and maintain comfortable eye contact with a sincere, friendly facial expression.

Use the correct amount of assertiveness – Have you ever wondered what causes family, friends and other prospects to dodge your calls, not show up at an appointment, or completely avoid any contact with you? This common scenario could easily be avoided if professionals would learn this one very important skill.

Assert means *the amount of force or effort used to make an opinion known*. I'm not simply talking about volume (loudness of speech).

You can assert your opinion about your MLM business or product too much with a loud voice or a soft voice, and it will cause the prospect to back away from your ideas. If your prospect can't hear you, your communication is worthless. If you talk too loudly so everyone in the lounge can hear you, you are being too assertive.

You can assert questions too repetitively and cause your prospect to feel interrogated. You can assert not enough and cause the prospect to feel your MLM business or product is not important.

When you master assertiveness, "You Have It." When the individual talks, people want to listen to him or her. When you have "it," prospects want to learn more about your MLM business. When you have "it," people will want to learn more about your great products.

When you have "it," your downline will want to follow you and duplicate your training.

Conversely, network marketing professionals who don't have "it" drive prospects away. People back away and won't buy your product or service, and your network marketing organization won't follow your suggestions. Perhaps the word that best describes "it" is "charisma." The definition of charisma is: a personal quality attributed to people who arouse devotion and enthusiasm.

When you have "it," your prospects want what you're offering. People want to be around you. People listen to what you say. If you don't have "it," you can use the exact same prospecting scripts as someone who has "it," but not have the same success. So this is a very important quality to have!

If you do not use the correct amount of assertiveness, you will waste prospects and destroy relationships.

Communicate easily – When a person is relaxed and has an easy time communicating with someone, your ideas are received easier and you also listen better. Here are some things to keep in mind when trying to make your communications easier:

- No tension – Try not to talk with a prospect when you have tension or fear
  - Not being prepared
  - Rejection
- No strain
- Don't sound rehearsed – This a turn off. If you are going to use scripts, be comfortable enough with them that you make them your own.
- Don't use fluff words:
  - un-believable
  - awesome
  - fantastic
  - great

  Nothing is wrong with being excited about what you have, just share what excites you.
- No stuttering
- Sound relaxed

Don't let your appearance or body scent distract the prospect – I am going to share some research that I found and thought was very interesting.

A survey was done at a very large trade show as people were walking out the door. They were asked a series of questions about the trade show.

Before I give you the answers to the survey, think about the money that companies invest in trade shows: the booth fee (sometimes tens of thousands of dollars), the travel, the display materials (sometime hundreds of thousands or even millions), accommodations and meal for the employees and sales reps that attend the trade show, etc.

One of the survey questions was "What's the number one reason you didn't buy today?" Guess what reason the prospects gave the most — the sales rep's bad breath! Can you believe that!?! The prospects didn't say the number one reason was because of a poor presentation or that the event wasn't exciting or anything else. The number one reason was bad breath!

The reaction to perfume and cologne is similar to bad breath. You may think your perfume makes you smell like a flower, but to someone else you might as well be wearing bug spray. You may even get compliments from some people, but that doesn't mean your specific prospect is going to love it.

People who wear perfume first put a dab on, and over time their nose becomes less sensitive to it. For them to smell it, they have to put two dabs, then three, and pretty soon you can smell those people coming IN the room — not when they've walked past you, but when they enter the room!

If this scent is something that prospects don't like they will be backing up (running away) trying to distance themselves from you. So, the rule is: MAKE SURE YOUR BODY DOESN'T DISTRACT YOUR PROSPECT.

The same rule applies to dress. Dress professionally. Ladies, if you have a beautiful body that you like to show off, that's great, but I don't recommend showing it off with prospects. Your body may get more of their attention than your business. The reason you're there is to be interested in them (more specifically the problem your business can solve for them), not to have them be interested in your body.

Now I know what some are thinking: "But people buy you, not the business or the product." This statement is very true. But what about you, do they buy? In network marketing, they buy your ability to help them get what they need or want as it relates to your business or product. If you dress provocatively and your prospects join the business because they like looking at you, you will have a tough time trying to keep them focused on the business. When you've concluded your business for the day and you want to dress up and wear perfume - great! But keep business and personal separate. Your dress code should be appropriate for the situation and the others present.

In my business, I work with people who like to travel. It's not appropriate to wear a suit or even dress clothes for that matter. Nice shorts and polo shirts get the best response. When we work in doctors' offices, we dress professionally but not in suits. In business presentations, suits work the best. The best rule of thumb is dress as nicely as the most nicely dressed guest.

From poorly tied ties to body odor, from odd behaviors like tapping your foot to putting on lipstick in front of your prospects, all can be distracting and cause them to focus their attention on something other than the thing that can help them achieve what they want.

And my final piece of advice on this topic is to make sure your breath is fresh!

Tell the truth – Whether you lead just a few or a few thousand people in your business, you must have this one very specific quality.

If you do not tell the truth, your downline may be friendly to you, but they probably won't follow you.

Much has been written about truth with a lot having to do with philosophy and religion. In this book, my only interest in the subject is that we, as an industry, stop destroying our income and our reputation by not telling the truth.

Throughout the various businesses I have had, at one time or another, I have seen my residuals crumble. I could not understand why.

After looking deeper into it, I noticed much of the growth was from a specific leg. As I dove even deeper, I noticed it lead to a specific organization.

Once I isolated the names, I began to make some phone calls and asked why these people dropped out. I would get the same response: "So and So told me this or So and So told me that. If it was not for that, I would have not joined." It was hard to believe that people were lying to others just to get them in the business. I have seen this time and time again.

I have not only seen this in my organization, but I have gone to outside meetings and observed the same. If you have been in this industry for any length of time, you know what I am talking about.

Let's talk about five reasons why individuals or a company does not reach full potential or eventually shuts down.

- False income representation or suggesting others can earn a stated level of income.
- Stating that a product or service can do something that has not been substantiated.
- Promising someone (or yourself) something and not doing it.
- Gossiping about others. Passing information to another that does not add value.
- Building the business in a way that is not truthful, such as suggesting distributors create fictitious accounts or positions.

As per the first point above (false income representation), if you don't know what your up-line earns, don't say what you think it is. If through the grapevine you've heard it's "X" amount, and you feel you must state it, say, "The rumor is that she earns $ _____; although I've not verified it." Say nothing you don't know is absolutely true. This gives you tremendous credibility!

When you discuss income, discuss what the prospect wants - NOT what someone else is earning. If prospects state an income they want, tell them it's doable here (provided it is). Then state, "Some people go to school and become the President. Some become billionaires, some sell illegal drugs, and some draw a welfare check. It would be impossible to know what you're going to do with what I teach you, but you have the potential to earn a substantial income if you choose to fully apply what you're taught."

The second point from above is unsubstantiated product claims, which have also gotten the network marketing industry into trouble in the past. If you market a nutrition product, the current law (in the USA) is the DSHEA Act (Dietary Supplement Health and Education Act), which states you can discuss what a product does, provided THE PRODUCT is what has been proven to get results.

Most often an INGREDIENT has had some studies done on it (such as vitamin C), but your company's product (that contains that ingredient) has NOT. Therefore, it is against the law to claim your product does ANYTHING!

Now, that doesn't mean you can't promote your product truthfully. You simply say something like "The active ingredient _____ in (an example of your company's product) has demonstrated to increase/decrease _____ by X amount." That way you're not claiming your product does anything.

Telling stories of your MLM success or others' success with the product or the business is also common. I'm not saying don't do it, nor am I saying to do it. Just keep in mind that the common way people get in trouble is from questionable claims reported by the media after coming in with hidden recording devices and capturing what you say. So, make sure you are not claiming anything that isn't the truth.

If a friend went on your company's product and stopped having migraine headaches, you honestly wouldn't know if the reason was the product or the fact that she increased her water intake to take your product! You can't determine what really helped her, so be very careful what you represent.

The third point above is to keep your word once it is given. If you say you will be at a meeting at 6:45, be there at 6:45. No excuses, just be there. If you say you're going to help someone, help them. Keep your word. If for some reason you're unable to keep your word, make it up to the person. Do something that shows you want to help.

When you're honest with yourself and with others, people will trust you. This trust is what helps your MLM business grow and be successful. My experience is that people will not follow someone they cannot trust. Tell the truth always and you will be on your way to experiencing passive income and time freedom in your MLM business.

And one last concluding thought that sums up this entire topic. The most important person you must keep your word with is yourself. If you say you are going to bed at 11pm, go to bed at 11pm. If you say you will call five prospects a day, call five prospects a day! We have spent quite a bit of time discussing how to get yourself to do what you tell yourself you will do during our topic on setting goals.

Know what you are talking about – Knowing your product or service is one of those skills that will place you above all others.

You could master the skill of salesmanship and effective communications, but if you do not know what you are talking about, you will lose a customer or distributor.

Think about the times you sat up late in the evening or early in the morning and started watching infomercials. You come across an infomercial that really captures your interest. Next thing you know, you are buying the item. Ever wonder why? It's because the presenter knew everything about that product. He answered all your questions before you could even think of them.

It's the same way in network marketing. If you present the proper information, use the tools provided to you, you will have less objections and more sign ups.

Remember, the last quality we talked about… TELL THE TRUTH.

Communicate at the prospect's level – Making your prospect feel dumb is probably the most counterproductive thing you can do when trying to get him into your business, yet so many people do it without knowing they do it.

When you communicate at the prospect's level, he "gets" you. He feels the two of you are on the same "wavelength." Failing to communicate at the prospect's level makes him feel dumb and like he can't do it. He also feels very "different" than you.

Have you ever sat around people speaking a different language? You felt alienated — and you were.

If you use *esoteric terms*, ("intended for or understood by only a particular group.") that your prospect doesn't know, then you're going to have partial or no communication. What does that mean?

> **Partial communication** is when parts of what you say are understood by the prospect and parts are NOT understood. An example is when you say "breakaway compensation plan." The prospect only understands "compensation plan" so he knows it has something to do with making money, but the exact meaning isn't clear to him.

> **No communication** is when you say something and the prospect has no idea what you're talking about. You say physiochemical (meaning nutrients in plants that have health-promoting properties) and they think "dog chemicals." You might think I'm exaggerating, but I'm not! I've surveyed people about what they think the term "Network Marketing" means. Six out of ten (60 percent) think it's something to do with selling computer networking equipment! That's NO communication.

You must communicate only with words that are in your prospect's vocabulary. If you really think about it, a dictionary merely describes an unknown word with words already in a person's vocabulary. That's the reason there are different levels of dictionaries - children's dictionary, collegiate dictionary, medical dictionary, and so forth.

Vocabulary — what does that word even mean? One definition is "all the words of a language." That definition would be good if everyone knew all words and all their definitions, but not everyone does. The second definition of the word vocabulary is "the sum of words used by, understood by, or at the command of a particular person." That's a much better definition for what we're discussing here.

So where did you get your current vocabulary? You got it from things you've heard or things you've read. Creating your own words doesn't do any good because no one knows what the words mean except you. A comparison is if you had the only fax machine in the world — who could you send a fax to?

Contrary to what your English professor told you, you do NOT become a great communicator because you have a large vocabulary alone. It's part of it, but not the whole package. A larger vocabulary allows you to communicate to a larger audience - meaning you have more in common with a greater number of people. It gives you diversity. Let's suppose you knew the entire English vocabulary. You could then carry on a conversation with anyone on any subject until you ran into someone who spoke Spanish. At that point, you would have no communication again. If you learned all the words of the Spanish language, then you could communicate to anyone in Spanish on any subject also.

What points am I trying to make here?

> First, good communication is not something one is born with. Every person had to learn the definition of all the words in their vocabulary.

> Second, you can communicate with people only to the degree that you know and use THE SAME vocabulary they do. If you knew all the words of a language, its value would only be known by the one other fellow who knew all the words.

Most of the time you will never use more than about 10% of your vocabulary because that's what most people know. And for you to be a good communicator, you MUST use words that the person you're communicating with knows. Otherwise that person will walk away from you, hang up the phone, fail the class that you're teaching, or quit network marketing! Don't think for a second that people will say they don't know something - even if you ask them if they understand.

A person will pretend to know something so he doesn't seem dumb. But he may be dumb on that word or subject and will forever stay that way because he would rather appear smart and be dumb, than be smart by asking, "What does that mean?" So don't use words people don't know. If you need to use a new word, only use words to define that new word that your prospect already knows. And please, please, please, when you hear something you don't understand, ask what it means.

Have the intention to make the person's life better – When inviting your prospect and communicating (selling) with your prospect, your intention needs to be focused on the correct thing if you want success in network marketing.

The definition of the word *intention* is "an aim that guides action." You could flip that around and also say that all past actions were preceded by an intention. For example, your intention was to go to the store; your action was to get in your car. Your action of getting in the car was based upon desiring to go to the store. Intention comes first, and then action follows.

If your intention with your prospect is correct, then your actions will be correct. When it comes to inviting someone to look at your network marketing business, your intention prior to the call, during the call - and as long as you know this person - should be to ***make the prospect's life better***. If your intention with your prospect is the wrong one, then your actions will reveal what your true intentions are. People often think they can fake it. I disagree.

If your aim is to truly make your prospect's life better, then everything you do should be towards that, and it will be obvious to the prospect. If your aim is to make money, make your monthly volume requirements, or get off the phone within three minutes, then everything you do will be towards that and obvious to the prospect also.

The point of this quality/attribute is to make sure your intention is pure and focused on ***making the prospect's life better***. If you do this, you will always say the right thing to that prospect.

The true advantage network marketing has over all other industries is our ability to really have a conversation with the prospect and find out what will make his life better. Telemarketers don't do this, advertisements on radio and television don't do this, and you won't find it in direct mail. But it's quite obvious to anyone who wants to look that we in network marketing can truly care and demonstrate that care by keeping the intention to make the prospect's life better throughout our conversation with them.

Chapter Seven

WHAT IS THE IMPORTANCE OF CUSTOMERS?

Why is it important to have customers or new distributors? This question is actually very simple. Why are you in business? You are in the business to make money, not just because it is something to do. Remember what your 'WHY" is (chapter 3)? Can you achieve it without new customers or distributors on your team? No.

Now, there is a process to gain new customers or distributors. No matter what type of business you are in, a process always exists. The process you must follow must be re-creatable. You, as either the salesman or recruiter, must be very familiar with this or you will fail. Many of you are already doing a form of the process we are going to discuss.

GREETING

Greeting – A word or gesture of salutation or expression to your prospect or customer. This could be non-verbal or verbal.

Non-verbal greeting
- Hand wave
- Smile
- Handshake

Purpose – The purpose of the greeting is to find out what your prospect needs and wants. In other words, your whole purpose is to just meet people.

- Not just a simple hello. It may just be a part of the greeting.
- The greeting is not over until you achieved the purpose of the greeting.
- If your prospect is not freely and openly talking to you, do not move on to the next step. If you jump to the next step (Qualify), then the greeting was not accomplished.
- Not just done face to face

How to greet correctly – Involves making statements and asking questions

- **Warm Market**
  - The greater you know someone, the more in-depth questions you can ask at the beginning.
  - Common error is to think about what to say next, while the prospect is answering your question.
  - People you know are more likely to answer your questions.

NOTE – Remember, just because you know them, it does not mean you jump right to qualifying them.

- **Cold Market (Strangers)** - Done on the phone or face-to-face. There are two ways to do it.
  - Start with a blunt question like, "Do you use a cell phone?"
    1) This way is just like a survey
    2) Not abrupt
  - Talk about items in the environment
    1) Does not just mean the weather, but your surroundings or observations
    2) Gets your prospect focused on the environment, not you trying to sell them something

Greetings turn into conversations, which turn into relationships. The more you talk, the more you find out the things you have in common. No relationship just happens, someone creates it.

Entities of a relationship –

- You
- Prospect
- Relationship – Requires the first two to exist. One starts and tries to build on it. Once the other starts to contribute, the relationship actually begins.

Greeting people from an advertisement – When you receive a lead from an advertisement or some other source lead, you are in the role of evaluating someone.

- You are in the position to go right to the "Qualifying" mode. But do not forgo the Greeting step.

  - Call the lead and inform him that you are calling in reference to _____.

- Ask him a few qualifying questions. If he is willing to talk, it will open you up for a proper greeting.

- This will allow you to find out more about the prospect, and find out what he wants in life.

- Ask questions like "What do you want in life?" or "What do you want to accomplish?" These questions will allow the prospect to open up freely.

Greeting from a purchased lead or lead capture page – It is important to know where the lead came from. This will allow you to evaluate not only the lead, but also the prospect.

- Open the call with asking for the person.

- Introduce yourself.

- Ask how they came across your site or if they filled out something online.

It is very important to qualify the lead itself. Some people just fill out forms to get something for free or job hunting. If the lead comes from a capture page you have created, you know the questions the form asked or what is on the site. Knowing this information will aid you in the interview process.

If the prospect remembers your site or filling something out online, then you can move into the "Greeting" step. If they do not remember, fish around to see if an interest exists. If not, thank them for their time, close out on a good note, leave your name and number, and end the call. This allows you to not waste time on a dead lead.

Since your intent with a greeting is to meet people and build relationships, then that's what your focus MUST be on. If your sole focus is to make sales or get distributors right off the bat, they will notice, and you will have little success. As your relationship builds, you will know if you can move on to the next step of "Qualifying" them.

Have fun just learning how to properly greet people and keep the focus on that. Once you have built a relationship with your prospect, then you can learn what his wants and needs are. Once you know what his wants and needs are, you can evaluate if you have something to make his life better. If you do, then move on to step 2.

QUALIFY

Qualify – To affirm capable and willing.

Purpose – To find out what the prospect needs, wants, and doesn't want pertaining to your business. This is the process of merging what the prospect wants and/or needs with what your business opportunity or product offers.

Merging the information – Know what the prospect's why is. This is more than just "I want to earn extra money or look younger." If you know the prospect's why, it will help you with the prospecting or sale. Educate your prospect on how your opportunity will help them achieve their want or need.

Qualifying questions – This is the process of finding out if your prospect's needs and wants can be met through your opportunity or product.

The person who keeps asking the questions controls the conversation. This is very important. You never want the prospect to take control.

What can be answered when asking questions:
- Can your product, service, or opportunity make your prospect's life better?
- Is the prospect looking for a job or a home-based business opportunity?
- Does your prospect mind working on commissions only?
- Is the prospect coachable, trainable and willing to listen?
- What is the prospect willing to do to create success?
- How much time does the prospect have to dedicate to his own business?
- How much is the prospect willing to invest in his own business?

These are just a few questions that will help you decide if the prospect qualifies for you to invite him to view your opportunity or product.

Working with purchased leads – Working with these leads are often the best, depending on the company and how many times the leads have been sold.

Depending on how the lead was captured, many of the qualifying steps are already done by just filling out the lead questionnaire.

It's up to you to go through the steps of still conducting a greeting and asking the qualifying questions that will show if you can meet the prospect's needs and wants.

Many people have designed scripts for this process.

Once you have either qualified or disqualified your prospect, the next step is to move to the "Invite Phase."

Chapter Eight

THE INVITE

Once you went through the process of finding out what your prospect's needs and wants are through the "Greeting," you then went through the "Qualify" process. This process allowed you to see if you had something that would meet the prospect's needs and wants and would make the prospect's life better. Also, you learned if the prospect had the qualities that are required to build a successful business. The next step is to get the prospect to view your opportunity. In network marketing you're inviting people to look at either the business or the product or both.

Business: This is where you show and educate your prospects about network marketing. Have them really understand and believe in its ability to provide adequate income and time freedom. Then show your product or service. This style is sometimes called "top down" or "business first."

Product: Show your prospects only the product (skin care, nutrition, telephone services, Internet services, etc.). After your prospect falls in love with the product, he'll know the business is viable. This style is called "bottom up" or "product first."

The lack of understanding of these two methods causes much frustration to those of us who are in network marketing and those who are not.

Invite – The word invite in the context that I'm using it is the act of asking someone to do something. Go to a movie, meet for breakfast, watch a video, etc.

Purpose – To ask your prospect to review information that can help them achieve what they need, want, or don't want.

During the "Qualify" phase, one of the questions you should have asked the prospect was "Do you have a problem working on commissions?"

If the prospect didn't, you should have showed them a video on network marketing. One of the two best videos I have seen are The Perfect Business by Robert Kyrosaki and Brilliant Compensation by Tim Sales. These videos go over the network marketing industry and direct sales.

When the "Qualify" process is done correctly, the "Invite" phase is a piece of cake. You use the relevant information gained from the "Qualify" phase.

STEPS TO INVITING

When talking with your prospect, use what his wants and needs are to move into the invitation to view your opportunity.

For example, if I was talking with a prospect named Shawn, I'd ask something like this — "Shawn, remember when you said your goal is to put your children through college?" After Shawn responds with an affirmative "yes," I would invite him to view a video or DVD re-emphasizing that I may have a way to help him achieve that goal.

No matter how you are going to expose a prospect to your opportunity (web video, DVD, or an opportunity meeting), make sure every prospect views one of the videos I mentioned above or one similar prior to your opportunity. These videos will prepare them for the type of opportunity you have.

After the prospect views the video, follow up and handle any questions or objections. When you have done that, you will eliminate many of the objections to network marketing or direct sales. The only questions being asked after that are "opportunity specific." Whenever a prospect has questions and objections, back up and handle them first. If you move on, you will be handling objections and questions not only about "The Industry," but also about your opportunity at the same time.

Once all the questions and objections are handled, if there were any, you want to "close to action." Get them to view your opportunity. If it is a face-to-face meeting or a business opportunity meeting, schedule that before you get off the phone.

There are times you will meet up with the prospect for a face-to-face introduction. If you don't have a video online they can view prior to viewing your opportunity, I would recommend having a laptop or mini DVD player. After you greet each other and engage in casual conversation, show them your DVD and then handle questions or objections. Once all questions are answered, "close to action."

You have now completed the invite phase. Remember, the "Qualify" phase is to see if you have something that will or will not meet the needs and wants of the prospect. And the "Invite" phase is to just get your prospect to view information that may help him achieve his goals.

Chapter Nine

HANDLING OBJECTIONS AND QUESTIONS

Network marketing is one of the most fun and rewarding businesses in the world, but eventually all network marketers are faced with certain widespread and universal challenges. No matter how long we participate in MLM and no matter how successful we become, we always run the risk of being temporarily shot down by the most prevalent and dangerous weapon of all — rejection. Rejection can and will strike any time, rendering us virtually immobile, thus destroying our enthusiasm and excitement, which are the essential qualities for success.

Just remember, you did not lose a prospect, but you gained a customer.

Objections are inevitable in any business – Many times, people make objections because they do not completely understand the information you have given them. If so, a clarification may be necessary. Others give objections because they are not accustomed to saying "Yes!" on the spot. They may think that they can find something wrong with your terrific home business. And yet other people may use objections as an excuse or because an objection is more comfortable for them than simply telling you "No." They don't want to hurt your feelings.

Regardless of the situation, you will feel more prepared to present your opportunity to others if you are armed with some appropriate responses to the potential objections you may encounter. After all, many studies have shown that what prevents us from approaching people about our business is not the fear of talking to other people and hearing "No," but the fear of not being able to answer their questions or counter their objections.

Purpose – The majority of the people you call will have one of the following questions or concerns. You need to expect these concerns and be prepared to immediately handle the questions or objections properly with a strong posture of certainty and confidence. The objective is not to create resistance, but to present logical and reasonable responses to their questions. Always keep in mind that your goal is to create curiosity and to get a firm commitment from the prospect to review your business. NEVER try to explain the opportunity over the telephone.

When answering questions, don't ramble. Be brief with your response and stay on track.

COMMON OBJECTIONS & APPROPRIATE RESPONSES

Question: "What is it?" or "Tell me more!" This is a natural response from someone after you have created curiosity. These people are not asking for full phone presentation. They are just curious. Here are some simple ways to handle this common question.

Response A: "Tom, I recognize the value of your time. And just as your time is valuable, so is mine. If this were something that could be effectively presented by phone, I certainly would; it would save both of us time, but it can't."

Response B: (If you're having resistance to Response A...) "Tom, if this business could be explained over the phone I would certainly try. You have to take a look at all the facts. The website will give you the picture in less than 15 minutes. Are you by your computer?"

Question: "Is it Amway, Shaklee, Melaleuca, Herbalife...?"

Response: No, _____, it is not like anything you have ever seen before." Then proceed to confirm an appointment.

Rejection: "I don't travel."

Response: "Do you pay taxes and/or want to earn extra income? Do you know anyone who takes vacations and/or travels, or anyone who wants to earn some extra income? If so, XYZ Company can still benefit you."

Rejection: "I don't have time."

Response: "How much time do you think it would take to save thousands of dollars a year on taxes? Former IRS Attorney Sandy Botkin says with a home-based business, three minutes a day can turn into as much as $5,000 or more per year in tax deductions.

Perhaps you could spend three minutes of your day that way, have more money in your pocket, and save some of the time you have to spend working now."

Rejection: "I don't have the money."

Response: "How does that make you feel? I understand. But what I've found is that people in America today who really want to be part of the XYZ program will find the money. If you receive a paycheck, your tax savings alone could give you an immediate pay raise. And if you become a Rep, I will work with you over the next four weeks to help you find seven people who want to become Reps. When you do, you will have earned back all of your set-up fee plus more, and XYZ Company will begin taking your monthly fee from profit not pocket. AND you'll enjoy thousands of dollars of savings each year."

Rejection: "I can't afford the monthly charge"

Response: "Do you pay a cell phone, cable, or utilities bill every month?" Help the prospect see how they can eliminate the monthly cost by showing them the 3x3 method. (See your up-line). Give the prospect something to think about.

Rejection: "I don't know anybody who would want to do this. I've tried everything and I don't want to go back to my friends again."

Response: "I understand, but you need to realize that XYZ Company is unique. As XYZ Company grows, someone will probably tell your friends about the program. Our experience is that people who would never join other programs will join XYZ because of the tremendous savings. And saving thousands is the equivalent of making thousands."

Rejection: "Is this MLM or network marketing?"

Again, this is generally an indication that your approach sounded dated and ordinary, like re-run "pitches" they've heard before. Start working on your own personal approach more.

Response A: "Yes, it is. What do you know about MLM or network marketing?

Response B: "Bob, I recognize you will have a lot of questions, just as I did. If this were something that could be effectively outlined over the phone, I would certainly do it; but it can't. That is why I need to get you to view my information on the internet."

Response C: "Joe, if this business were just an ordinary network marketing company, I wouldn't be interested either. This is something that's honestly different! Let's get you into the information. Are you by your computer? I think you'll be as impressed as I am." Proceed to confirm the appointment.

Rejection: "I'm not interested!" (This is a definitely an indication you told your prospect too much.)

Response: "Bob, would you be willing to at least do me a favor?" (Sure) "Would you take just 15 minutes and go through the website. The information is compelling and I would hate to leave you behind. I'm forming my team of TOP GUNS and want you to be on it."

Rejection: "I don't like MLM. I've lost money and been burned on everything I've tried."

Response: "If you lose money in XYZ, it's because you choose to. The thing that totally sets XYZ apart from other companies is that our agents save thousands of dollars on vacations and potentially thousands more on taxes. Whether you build the MLM portion or not is irrelevant to your saving money. If you never even try to sponsor anyone, you will have gotten an incredible value, and you can still send people to your website to book travel and earn money that way. Everyone wins with XYZ!"

Rejection: "I've got to go home and talk with my spouse."

Response A: "That's a great idea. All I ask is this: please don't try to explain our program. Let's set up a time, and I will show him/her the same presentation that you had the advantage of seeing. That way, he/she will understand the program and together you can make an informed decision."

Response B: "I agree with you that our spouses' support is necessary. Could we talk with your spouse together?

Rejection: "You can't possibly legally save that kind of money on taxes!"

Response: "I know how you feel. I felt the same way. But when I put myself in front of the information taught by tax experts, such as former IRS attorney Sandy Botkin, I realized that millions of Americans are saving thousands of dollars on taxes each year with a home-based business. And an added benefit to XYZ is that you can legitimately deduct your travel and vacation expenses. It's not that we can't do it... it's just that not everybody knows about it! Once I learned about the tax advantages, I decided right then to join the millions who can legally and ethically reduce their taxes. Check with your CPA, and I'm sure he/she will validate all of this for you."

Rejection: "This sounds like one of those pyramid scams."

Response A: "Please explain to me what you think a pyramid is. A pyramid is the foundation of corporate America. No one below the CEO makes more than he/she. No one below the President makes more than them and so forth, you can see the pattern." Also, "Do you see Carnival Cruises, FunJet Vacations, and Hertz Car Rental being associated with an illegal company?"

Response B: "George, do you think I would be involved in an illegal pyramid?"

Response C: "George, no, this is a company that provides the latest technology in leisure travel solutions. It is capitalizing on the greatest trend in the industry. The company has a track record of exploding success. I'm part of a team that is in charge of national expansion. Are you by your computer?"

NOTE: If you are feeling some resistance from your prospect, you may want to try using the TAKE-AWAY APPROACH.

EXAMPLE 1: "Bob, when I looked at who could most benefit from this business, I immediately thought of you. If you are not interested in taking a brief look at it, that's okay. I was just thinking of you."

EXAMPLE 2: "Allen, all I want to accomplish in this brief phone conversation is to see if you have an interest in taking a look at a new business venture. If this is the wrong time in your life, that's fine. I was just thinking of you. I thought if it were the right time in your life, you are the kind of person I would enjoy working with."

Rejection: "I don't like giving out my personal information"

Response: "That's why we made it convenient to go to our website, click join, and fill out your application in the privacy of your own home."

Chapter Ten

PRESENTING YOUR PRODUCT AND OPPORTUNITY

What we have learned leads up to this point, the actual sharing of your product or opportunity. This is what you have been building up to. It is time to get your prospect to a presentation.

Tips to a successful presentation – Several things determine the success of a presentation, no matter what the topic. To most, they are extremely obvious, but often completely overlooked. What makes a presentation great, instead of average (or sometimes even painful), are the little details that we often take for granted.

Sometimes what we think will guarantee our success will eventually lead to failure. For example, many people think that the best way to prepare a speech or presentation is to memorize it word for word. What most people don't realize is that this method is extremely unreliable.

Surprisingly, when someone memorizes a speech or presentation, they often forget the entire speech when they face the audience. This has happened to countless distinguished public figures, even Winston Churchill!

Another reason memorization isn't a recommended method is that the presentation will have a stiff, lifeless tone. Dale Carnegie points out that all of our lives we have been speaking spontaneously. Carnegie says, "We haven't been thinking of words; we have been thinking of ideas. If our ideas are clear, the words come as naturally and unconsciously as the air we breathe."

Keeping your ideas clear and concise is another key. This is particularly important when developing your visual aids and presentation materials. When creating a PowerPoint presentation, it is important to keep things crisp and uncluttered. Often, too many graphics, long phrases, and other distracting items on the slides make it very difficult to obtain and keep the audience's attention.

Handouts are an essential tool in working-up a successful presentation. By giving the audience the material, they will spend more time listening and absorbing information, instead of scrambling to capture notes on paper. Many speakers will reserve their handouts until the end of the presentation, but this annoys many attendees because they like to jot down notes as the speaker presents the material.

Take a few moments before your session begins by stopping by the meeting room, familiarizing yourself with the equipment and location of items you may need at the last minute. By doing this, you will be able to avoid the stress of adapting to new and possibly unfamiliar equipment. Also, this will help you ensure that all equipment is working properly. Feel free to practice using the microphones or other aides.

Take a few moments to relax and mentally prepare yourself for the presentation you are about to give. Quickly review your notes and go over any sticking points or places you feel you need to clarify.

HOME PRESENTATIONS

It is important to keep meetings (parties) simple. From the time you pick up the phone, they're in training. No full course dinners, etc. Remember, you want people who come to see that they can do this, too. So, plan on having soft drinks/coffee and a bag of cookies or chips. Home parties are a great way to put people into your business or sell your product. They are one of the fastest ways to grow your team and are a great way to build your team along with moving product.

Your list - Go to the list of names you have and invite everyone to your house party. Make sure you have them RSVP, so you'll have an idea of how many people are going to attend your Grand Opening.

The day before your meeting - The day before the meeting, call back the people who said yes and confirm that they will be there. One good way to keep someone to their word is to ask them to bring a bag of ice. Explain that you have been so busy that you have fallen short. Then ask the next people to bring some chips. Most people, when they obligate themselves to bring something, will keep to their promise. We have had 10 bags of ice sitting in our tub in the past. Keep in mind that there may still be some attrition (some people will back out), but keep calling everyone who said they would come. Those who back out can be scheduled for the next party/meeting or another meeting you can set up for the following week. People are busy and sometimes a reminder is all that's needed to increase attendance.

Use the following structure:

- Schedule your sponsor or up-line leader — or a business "expert" — to help you with your party even if they have to be on the phone to do so.

- Invite twice as many people as you expect to attend by saying to them, "I've found a fabulous way to save thousands of dollars on XYZ. It's so much fun! I'm having a party next _____ night at 7:30. Can you attend?" When they reply "Yes," say, "This is very important to me. I know I can count on you coming. What could possibly come up that might cause you to have to cancel?"

- On the night of the party, have music playing when guests arrive. Ensure the music is appropriate for the setting.

- Keep the party fun and lively with light refreshments as said above.

• Begin by welcoming everyone and showing them your recent vacation pictures (if you're in the travel business).

• Get them to participate by asking questions, such as "Who is interested in going to that particular destination?" or ask if they know someone who has been there. The purpose is getting them to sell themselves on the opportunity or product.

• Show your presentation.

• When you finish — call your up-line leader or "expert" and they will answer your prospects' questions and close them.

Closing your presentation – This is the most important part of your presentation. Whether you are trying to close a prospect on the phone following an online presentation, in person one-on-one, or at a party, closing is THE most important part of the presentation. Without a strong close, all of the work that you have done can be wasted. All that is required to develop a strong close is to use the following techniques and practice — practice — practice!

Ask Your Prospects What They Like Most. Fortunately, closing the presentation is simple — after all, it's simply asking your prospects what they like most about XYZ company, answering their questions and/or objections, and asking them to sign up.

Here are the steps:

Following the presentation, find out which aspect of your company or product interests them most.

• Are they interested in saving on …….?
• Are they interested in saving on taxes?
• Are they interested in making extra income?
• Or are they interested in a combination of the above?
• Answer their questions or objections.

- Ask them to sign up and join XYZ by focusing on what interests them.

"It Made Sense to Me" Close – One great closing technique is to simply say, "It made sense to me." Here is how you would use this closing technique:

- For prospects interested in travel: "When I saw this program and realized that I could save on my own travel by earning commissions on my vacations and travel, it made all the sense in the world to me to get started immediately. What do you think?" And — then be quiet and listen to their response.

- For prospects interested in tax savings: "When I saw this program and realized that I could save so much money each year on my taxes, it made all the sense in the world to me to get started immediately. What do you think?" And — then be quiet and listen to their response.

- For prospects interested in making extra income: "When I saw this program and realized that I could make some extra money by referring people to my own website and by sharing this program with others, it made all the sense in the world to me to get started immediately. What do you think?" And — then be quiet and listen to their response.

"Great Idea" Close – Another effective close is the "Great Idea" close. Here is how you would use this closing technique:

- For prospects interested in being a distributor: "I've got a great idea. Let's get you signed up tonight so that you can get started earning commissions on your personal purchases!" Then be quiet and listen to their response.

- For prospects interested in tax savings: "I've got a great idea. Let's get you signed up tonight so that you can begin saving on your taxes immediately!" Then be quiet and listen for their response.

- For prospects interested in making extra income: "I've got a great idea. Let's get you signed up as a representative tonight so that you can begin making some extra income immediately!" Then be quiet and listen for their response.

Tip: If you are recruiting long-distance, an effective technique is to ask, "Do you want to go online and sign up, or shall I fax you an application?" Whichever of these closing techniques you use, PRACTICE — PRACTICE — PRACTICE and you will sign people up!

SAMPLE SCRIPT

Name, (just say their name. Do not say Hello, Hi, or " Is Name?")
This is <Your Name>. (optional - calling from <Your City>)

How are you doing today? (Listen, comment, & move on quickly.)

I am just making a quick courtesy call. I see here that you requested some information on my website about earning extra money from home. (Do not pause.) ***Now are you looking for something full time or part time?*** (Listen.....)

(Comment and move on)

JOB - ***What are you currently doing for a living?*** (Listen, comment, & move on quickly.)

- ***What do you like best/least about being a*** <the job title>?
- ***How long have you been working in*** <the business field>?

REASON - ***What prompted you***, Name, ***to start looking online to earn extra money?***

TO HELP - ***So are you looking mainly for some extra income? Or are you looking more for the time freedom?***

AMOUNT - ***How much*** (extra if they said part time) ***are you looking to earn in dollars and cents on a monthly basis?*** (Wait for an answer, and then say...) ***Now is that just to get you to ground zero? Or would that make a positive financial impact on your life?*** (If they say, "Positive impact," move on. If they say, "Ground zero," then ask...) ***Well, how much would it take in dollars and cents on a monthly basis for you to really see the positive impact in your life? It is okay to dream a little.***

REPEAT IT – *Okay, so* <amount of money / month> *would really allow you to start enjoying life a little more.*

ELICIT DREAMS – (must get their dreams, most important) – the secret

So far we talked a little bit about what you need. Now let's talk about what you really want. Is that okay with you? Let me ask you a quick question, if time and money were not an object, what are some things you would want more of in life? What would you do with your spare time?

NOW THE PROCESS: Ask clarifying questions. Get the details. Do not assume anything.

Where would you like to _____? (If they answered travel earlier, ask if it for personal or business.) *Are you doing this now?*

So you want to go back to some of the places you really enjoyed on your own terms, right?

COMMIT – CREATE URGENCY

Wow, <Name>*! I'm getting really excited because based on what you told me, you are a lot closer to* (What they just told you above) *than you think.*

Now, <Name>, *if I had a video that would get you to* _____, *would you be willing to invest 20 minutes of your time?*

Now can you do that tonight? (Wait for answer. If the response is yes …) *What time will you be able to watch that tonight?* (If the response is no …) *Okay, when will you be able to watch it?*

PLAN FOLLOW-UP

So <Name>, *you are going to have some questions. What I want you to do is while you're watching the movie, keep a pen and paper handy so you can jot down the questions. I want to get to your questions while they are still fresh in your mind, so I will call you at* _____ . (Suggest a time about 30 minutes after the above agreed on time.) (Wait for commitment.)

Is this the phone number (repeat the phone number) *you want me to call you at* (agreed on time)*?*
Excellent! I look forward to speaking with you (tonight or tomorrow) *on the phone at* (time)

2ND CALL BACK TO PROSPECT
TO HEAR THE BUSINESS BRIEFING CALL

Call at the scheduled time of their business briefing. Call to give them their special invitation number.

Hello! May I speak to _____ *?... Hi* _____ , *this is* <Your Name> *from* <Your Business>. *We spoke* (earlier today or yesterday) *about you generating income from the comfort of your home.*
I wanted to give you the Special Invitation Number for tonight's business briefing.

Grab the paper you wrote on before and a pen. Let me know when you are ready? Okay! Here is the number to call, 555-555-5555.

As soon as we finish this call, you should get in a quiet room where you can focus and jot down any questions you may have during the Business Briefing call.

I will be receiving several calls right after the briefing is over.

So, if you are like me and get excited by what you hear…. (and you have questions, want more information, or you simply want to get started…) (Slow) **Call me right after the briefing. You may want to catch me before someone else does. If I miss your call or don't hear from you, then I will call you back when I get done enrolling the people that are ready to get started, okay? I look forward to speaking with you after the briefing. Bye for now!**